Engaging First-Year Students in Meaningful Library Research

CHANDOS
INFORMATION PROFESSIONAL SERIES

Series Editor: Ruth Rikowski
(email: Rikowskigr@aol.com)

Chandos' new series of books is aimed at the busy information professional. They have been specially commissioned to provide the reader with an authoritative view of current thinking. They are designed to provide easy-to-read and (most importantly) practical coverage of topics that are of interest to librarians and other information professionals. If you would like a full listing of current and forthcoming titles, please visit www.chandospublishing.com or email wp@woodheadpublishing.com or telephone +44(0) 1223 499140.

New authors: we are always pleased to receive ideas for new titles; if you would like to write a book for Chandos, please contact Dr Glyn Jones on email gjones@chandospublishing.com or telephone number +44(0) 1993 848726.

Bulk orders: some organisations buy a number of copies of our books. If you are interested in doing this, we would be pleased to discuss a discount. Please contact us on email wp@woodheadpublishing.com or telephone +44(0) 1223 499140.

Engaging First-Year Students in Meaningful Library Research

A practical guide for teaching faculty

MOLLY R. FLASPOHLER

CHANDOS
PUBLISHING

Oxford Cambridge New Delhi

Chandos Publishing
Hexagon House
Avenue 4
Station Lane
Witney
Oxford OX28 4BN
UK
Tel: +44 (0) 1993 848726
E-mail: info@chandospublishing.com
www.chandospublishing.com

Chandos Publishing is an imprint of Woodhead Publishing Limited

Woodhead Publishing Limited
80 High Street
Sawston
Cambridge CB22 3HJ
UK
Tel: +44 (0) 1223 499140
Fax: +44 (0) 1223 832819
www.woodheadpublishing.com

First published 2012

ISBN: 978-1-84334-640-1 (print)
ISBN: 978-1-78063-294-0 (online)

© M. Flaspohler, 2012

Typeset by RefineCatch Limited, Bungay, Suffolk
Printed in the UK and USA.

This book is dedicated to Barb, Erika, Amy and Lisa T. Without these remarkable, intelligent and unfailingly cool women, I never would have gotten myself into this.

Contents

List of figures and table

Figures

Table

Foreword

Barbara Fister,
Gustavus Adolphus College

All of us feel overwhelmed, at one point or another, by the seemingly unstoppable accumulation of mail in our inboxes, the stream of news coming at us from so many directions, often feeding yet more news across cryptic flowing banners, the mysterious switchbacks we encounter as we navigate common medical advice – that thing that was good for you? It's not, after all – and the frustration of hearing two equally passionate sides to every debate, when we know the truth doesn't come in neat binaries. Information is too much with us, and too much of it is trivial or dubious or drawn from unconvincing evidence. But when we need to figure things out, we do the research.

Those of us teaching first-year college students usually confront another problem that also feels overwhelming at times. Students have always had trouble writing research papers, but on top of the usual culprits – choosing topics that are too narrow or too broad, providing a data-dump rather than an analysis, misusing words, splicing sentences together with commas when they aren't fragmenting them – we have to help them find their way through an abundant but increasingly complex information environment. Instead of going to the library, students go to Google, where scholarly sources, advocacy, government documents, personal narratives, news sources, scans of nineteenth-century books, and home-made videos are all shelved together, millions upon millions of documents available on any topic. If students are savvy enough to turn to the library's website, they are likely to search an aggregated database that includes more articles from more journals than any undergraduate library previously subscribed to. They have endless choices to make, but they can't fall back on a scaffold of understanding that more experienced scholars take for granted. They don't know the simplest things: that books have indexes, and that by using an index or table of contents they could get information from a book without having to read it cover-to-cover. They probably have never seen a scholarly journal in print, and don't realize such periodicals are published serially. They think 'argument' means a fight to the finish, not developing a reasoned position based on evidence. And they aren't sure, but they think *Time* magazine is what their teacher means when they say 'use scholarly sources.'

Lacking experience with traditional research tools is one thing; they also lack experience with developing researchable questions, drawing conclusions from evidence, examining sources critically, or having their minds changed when confronted with data that conflicts with their preconceptions. And (though this is nothing new) they lack a sense of urgency or commitment to doing research. A research assignment is just another jump-through-the-hoops demonstration for their teacher, another checkpoint that will show they did their homework, however grudgingly. An efficient strategy for getting through a research assignment with a minimum of effort, though rarely an effective one, is viewed as a survival skill, and rather than learn new ways to find out about the world, students will almost always draw on whatever tools and strategies they have used in the past. They are busy people; they don't have time to mess around. The fact that their college has a vast library of resources and their teachers have high expectations doesn't budge them from their course. Google has worked before, and everyone knows essays should be five paragraphs long. Come up with something to say, find a few sources to support it, and you're done. That shouldn't take more than a few hours, right?

The research paper remains the most common writing assignment on college campuses, more popular than ever (Lunsford, 2008). In the first year, just as students are encountering the conventions of academic writing, we also hope to ground them in the mechanics of using a print/digital hybrid library, probably much larger than any they've ever used before, to make informed choices among possible sources, and extract meaning from them in order to support a well-organized synthesis or argument. We know they will be asked to do this in the future, so we try to get them acculturated quickly.

This puts a lot of responsibility on those who teach first-year students the ropes of academic writing. Many instructors are dismayed to find, when they collect drafts of papers, that the library tour they scheduled in the second week of the course seems to have had no effect at all. No matter how much detail they put into the assignment prompt describing how to recognize high-quality sources, the bibliographies are full of sites from About.com and Knowledge Quest. And worst of all, the students seem already jaded, indifferent to the thrill of the hunt or the opportunity to pursue a question they care about. Yet apart from preparing inexperienced students for college, instructors know that these skills are for life. We need citizens that can find and interpret information, that respect evidence, that are prepared to question assumptions and ask the right questions. We know what happens in that first year matters. And it's not easy.

This book, written by an experienced academic librarian, is for every first-year instructor who has tried semester after semester to refine their research activities with students, only to be defeated by a new crop of novices. It's for every teacher who is puzzled by students who seem so savvy about technology, but so incapable of using it for academic purposes. It's for every librarian who wants to work more effectively with the faculty who help new students negotiate an unfamiliar and challenging set of expectations. It's for anyone who cares about the success of those first-year students.

Molly Flaspohler, who has observed students' confusion from the front lines of their forays into research and who has collaborated successfully with faculty to make research a more meaningful opportunity for learning, presents a well-organized and entertaining review of what we know about how students today approach research assignments, suggests how (and why) librarians and teaching faculty should collaborate fruitfully, and offers practical, experience-tested pedagogical approaches to introducing reluctant researchers to the intellectual work of articulating questions and seeking evidence-based solutions, work that can turn novice researchers into engaged students, ready to take the next step in their academic journey.

Work cited

Lunsford, Andrea A. and Karen J. Lunsford (2008) '"Mistakes are a Part of Life": A National Comparative Study.' *College Composition and Communication* 59.4: 781–806.

About the author

Molly R. Flaspohler currently serves as Special Projects Librarian at the Carl B. Ylvisaker Library located on the campus of Concordia College, Moorhead, MN. Over the past 20 years, she has held various positions within this library, including that of Library Instruction Coordinator and Chair of Reference Services. In her present role, Molly provides library instruction, reference services and departmental liaison support to the members of Concordia's Division of Language, Literature and Culture (English, French, German and Spanish and Hispanic Studies) as well as the Women's Studies program.

After obtaining a BA degree in English at Gustavus Adolphus College in St Peter, MN, a Master's of Library Science degree from the School of Library and Information Science at Bloomington, IN, and later, a Master's of Liberal Arts degree from Minnesota State University Moorhead, MN, Molly began her professional career as jack-of-all-trades. In her first library position, she was responsible for cataloging, reference desk service and library instruction. In 1994, she became Concordia College's first Coordinator of Library Instruction. In this role Molly taught hundreds of undergraduate library sessions and began several collaborations with teaching faculty which continue today. Ultimately, she was responsible for the Library's earliest attempts at integrating library instruction into the College's first-year composition courses in a more cohesive and systematic way. In 2005, Molly became the Chair of Reference Services. Though her primary responsibilities shifted to supervising student workers and paraprofessionals in the provision of excellent reference services, her work in the classroom remained a significant component of this position as well.

During 2007–08, Molly served as a visiting Associate Librarian at the University of Washington, Bothell/Cascadia Community College Library in Bothell, WA. This position, held as part of a year-long sabbatical leave, afforded a rich opportunity to work within a much larger university library system and to observe and engage in interesting, innovative ways to present undergraduate library instruction. After returning to Concordia, Molly soon applied for and was accepted into the Association of College and Research Libraries' well-known Teacher Track Immersion Program, which she completed over the summer of 2010.

Over the years, Molly has served on numerous College committees and task forces, including the College's First-Year Experience Task Force (2003), the First-Year Curriculum Committee (2004), two terms on Concordia's Faculty Senate, Curriculum Review (Team I), and the College Strategic Planning Commission (2002). Presently, she is a member of Concordia's campus-wide Assessment Committee. She is active in her profession as well, having presented at library conferences such as the Minnesota Library Association Annual Conference (2004), LOEX (2007) and LOEX of the West (2008). She has also published articles in peer-reviewed journals such as *Reference Services Review, Communications in Information Literacy* and *The Journal of Academic Librarianship*. Molly maintains memberships in the American Library Association and the Association of College and Research Libraries.

The author may be contacted at:

Carl B. Ylvisaker Library
Concordia College
901 8th St. So.
Moorhead, MN 56562
USA
E-mail: *mflaspoh@cord.edu*

Introduction

Abstract: Today's first-year undergraduate students are dreadfully ill-equipped to complete even the most basic academic research tasks. Citing real-life situations, this chapter introduces readers to the significant yet oft-ignored educational difficulties that such a lack of information literacy regularly creates. This chapter also outlines the pedagogical purposes of this text and offers further background about the variety of complex information obstacles faced by today's incoming undergraduates. Finally, this chapter provides a brief outline of the book's overall structural organization.

Key words: introduction, purpose, background, organization, library research, undergraduates, first-year students, novice researchers, Millennials, research paper failure, information literacy, teaching faculty, librarians.

Roughly two weeks prior to the end of this academic year, a young student reluctantly approached the library's Reference Desk where I work a number of hours per week. The first thing I noticed was that she had nothing with her that indicated she was planning to spend any time actually working in the library. She had none of the usual student accessories: no backpack, no assignment sheets, no textbooks, no tablet, no writing utensils, nothing. She simply walked up to the desk empty-handed and asked in a small voice, 'Can you tell me if this library has, uhm, like, a section

1

on prejudice?' The breadth of her query was more than enough to set off librarian alarm bells. But, figuring in the time of year at which such a vague question was being asked also meant that this student was likely to have only a week or less to complete what I eventually learned was to be a ten to fifteen-page research paper. This student should have been a great deal further along in her research process if she had any hope whatsoever of writing a paper that was anything more than a superficial data-dump.

A few days later, ten minutes before my final evening reference shift for the year ended, another student strode purposefully up to the desk and declared the following: 'I'm doing research on homosexual men in China, with a primary focus on the decade 1960 to 1970 and I was, like, wondering if there was a book on that in the library.' Upon seeing what must have been a relatively stunned look on my face (the academic library at which I work is small and the probability of locating a book with such topic specificity was unlikely at best), this student huffily added yet another criterion. 'Oh, and will this book be located here in the library for me to check out; because I do NOT intend to spend ANY more time in this building tonight.'

These two eleventh-hour requests illustrate a type of inquiry that is all too familiar to librarians who work with contemporary undergraduates at institutions of higher education. Alison Head and Michael Eisenberg (2009) think that reference questions such as these are evidence of the difficulty novice researchers have understanding the 'big picture context' of their research. Such a perspective involves not only selecting and describing a relevant topic but, 'understanding multiple sides of an argument' and 'figuring out how the topic might best fit into the course curriculum' (Head and Eisenberg, 2009: 6). Beyond being unable to locate the necessary information tools, the two students above seriously underestimate the time it takes to read, evaluate, compare, reflect upon, and/or effectively use library resources in order to create the kind of new meaning expected by their professors. While their reference questions are certainly asked from opposite ends of the specificity spectrum, both students' queries highlight obstacles faced by typical undergraduates as they attempt to identify and define their academic information needs. Once stuck, both students are neither experienced nor persistent enough to locate information that might help them adequately meet the requirements of their assignments.

Sadly, these two undergraduates appear to be ill-equipped for accomplishing meaningful library research in several ways. After further discussion with each of them, I learned that prior to approaching the reference desk neither had done any searching among *library* materials. Both students had rummaged around the Internet for some time despite having been specifically required to use library sources by their professors. Neither student appeared to have any knowledge of, nor desire to learn about the library's online catalog nor any of our other electronic databases. Both claimed not to even know how to get started researching with library-based tools. Finally, neither undergraduate understood how their search terms would influence the breadth or depth of their results. For example, student number one wanted to search for resources about 'prejudice' (which, incidentally, she didn't know how to spell correctly). Using only this extremely broad term would mean that this student's searches (no matter where she did them) would result in overwhelmingly enormous amounts of information, much of it irrelevant to what she actually may have been trying to find. Student number two was overly specific, inflexibly so. In a small library, such as the one she had to use, this student was likely to have great difficulty finding anything about such a rigidly narrow topic (attitudes toward male homosexuality in China during 1960–1970), particularly if she continued to insist upon typing in all of her search criterion together at once.

Both of these students make critical research errors common to many undergraduates and further exacerbate what is already a stressful situation by not allowing themselves enough time to really explore (i.e., closely read) information sources that are relevant, reliable and reputable. What is especially disheartening for these two undergraduates is that while the first was still new to campus, having yet to complete her first year in college, the second was well along in her postgraduate career. She was, in fact, nearing the end of her junior year. Despite the reasonably good first-year library instruction program offered at this institution, and likely exposure to at least one or two additional library sessions, neither the second student nor the first demonstrated an acceptable level of information literacy competency.

Sadly, their research experiences are far from unique, according to one recent study:

> No matter where students are enrolled, no matter what information resources they may have at their disposal, and no matter how much time they have, the abundance of information technology and the proliferation of digital information resources make conducting research uniquely paradoxical: Research seems to be far more difficult to conduct in the digital age than it did in previous times. (Head and Eisenberg, 2009: 2)

Today's students consider the Internet their library. Because using the Internet is fast, entertaining and filled with vast amounts of information, many students have come to see research as an easy, quickly accomplished task. Both students above gravely underestimate their ability to locate, evaluate and effectively use high-quality information sources, precisely because today's advanced information technology exists.

Purpose

In an introduction to her edited work, *Integrating Information Literacy into the Higher Education Curriculum: Practical Models for Transformation*, Ilene Rockman points out that although most students today can 'send electronic mail, chat, and download music,' the majority have no idea 'how to effectively locate information; evaluate, synthesize, and integrate ideas; use information in original work or give proper credit for information used' (2004b: 10). If you are a member of the professoriate or the library profession you are liable to be more familiar with this contemporary dilemma than you want to be. Today's Millennial students arrive at colleges and universities after having spent their entire childhoods immersed in developing technologies and having learned little or nothing about effectively using such devices in a scholarly research setting. These students come with cell phones equipped to do much more than simply talking with friends (texting, searching the Internet, checking e-mail, etc.), MP3 players with enormous media storage capacities, startlingly well-equipped laptops, Facebook accounts they have been using for years, and IM contact lists twice the size of most CEOs' Rolodexes. These young adults Skype, Twitter and Flickr their way into our classrooms and yet have an incredibly difficult time understanding why it may not be the best idea to base an entire college-level paper on an Internet website for which their only evaluative criterion was that it looked 'professional' and that it 'had a lot of information.' The subtext for these particular criteria, by the way, often has more to do with the fact that the student was ultimately pressed for time and the website was easy to find. Rather than spend precious time considering authorship, accuracy, currency or bias, many undergraduate researchers use websites because those that parrot their own views are easy to find and immediately available.

While it is true that the Millennials come to higher education having more access to information than any previous generation, many do not seem to know how to effectively utilize these opportunities in their new academic situations. Practically speaking, what this means is that teaching faculty and academic librarians recurrently encounter the first-year student who writes a paper on 'Olestra,' using only data gathered from Procter & Gamble's website; the undergraduate who asks if a librarian can help her find a few sources to add to her bibliography for a paper that she's *already written*; and the novice who asks for help with a list of 20 to 25 incomplete citations that she reluctantly admits were provided by *her mother*, who thought they were books this student should use for her project.

Based on a multiplicity of researched paper failures, those in higher education know only too well that new students do not arrive on our campuses demonstrating careful critical thinking abilities, savvy research proficiencies or, in many cases, even adequate time management skills. We also know that if these young adults are going to be knowledgeable, thoughtful and engaged citizens upon graduation, we better do something about this state of affairs. As one researcher emphasizes, 'It is not enough for adults to leave young people to get on with it [becoming information literate], but rather it demands that they [adults] listen and respond carefully, providing feedback on creative or other forms of activity, encouraging critical reflection, taking their [students] participation seriously' (Livingstone, 2008: 116). According to another study, this active adult intervention in the information literacy process may actually be better received by students than we initially expect. Meyers, Fisher and Marcoux (2009) report that when they discussed 'everyday-life information problems with tweens' these students felt that it was 'access to other *people* that often makes or breaks an information search' (337, emphasis added). While our students may have spent endless hours engrossed with technologies capable of things we of earlier generations could only dream of, most young people still appear to be open to learning from adults who take them and the technological skills they do have seriously.

Taking on the shared educational mission of information literacy is a great opportunity for teaching faculty and librarians to work together in new and innovative ways. If, together, we create and plan course-work that is challenging, engaging and important to our newest students, we can teach them to become careful thinkers and conscientious information users. Such collaborative work is likely to be rewarding for teaching faculty, academic librarians and new students alike. William A. Orme, an associate librarian at Indiana University-Purdue, has written that 'it is incumbent on members of the higher education community to explain the new culture and the unique and central role that information plays in the academic culture' to students who are new to the academy (2008: 69). It is, therefore, with this shared purpose in mind that *Engaging First-Year Students in Meaningful Library Research: A Practical Guide for Teaching Faculty* was first envisaged.

This volume is primarily meant to serve either as a resource for new instructors fresh from graduate school or as a tool for teaching faculty looking for ways to further integrate contemporary information literacy competencies into their first-year courses by refreshing their library-based pedagogical strategies. The book is intended to encourage teaching faculty to intentionally consider collaborations with their own academic librarians, so, as Orme puts it, together we might more 'synergistically develop the information abilities and enhance the academic experience of those who are entering a new intellectual community as they enroll in their first year of college' (2008: 63). This text also promotes the value of a process-driven, constructivist framework as a means of engaging novice researchers in library work that is interesting, meaningful and disciplinarily relevant. Therefore, the text has two overarching goals: to discuss the necessity and value of incorporating information literacy competencies into first-year courses; and also to provide a variety of practical, targeted strategies for doing so.

Background

Because today's Millennial generation has been almost entirely defined by their all-embracing use of technology, they are regularly credited with research skills that they do not possess. Faculty members who are new to their positions often have unrealistically heightened expectations of their first-year students' abilities to locate, evaluate and effectively use information. Even faculty members who have been in the classroom for some time can fail to recognize the limits of their newest students' research abilities.

Faculty members, no matter how concerned they are about their students, have not been undergraduates for a long time, and they have often forgotten what their own undergraduate experience was like. They are used to sophisticated discussions about research with colleagues, and in this environment it is all too easy to make assumptions about the level of understanding possessed by undergraduates (Leckie, 1996: 203).

Academic librarians frequently get caught in the middle of this disconnect. It happens when new students bring assignments to us with intentionally vague or extremely open-ended instructions (e.g., pick a topic related to some aspect of the environment and research it). It happens when faculty refer brand-new undergraduates to complex, advanced disciplinary indexes which provide information that these students aren't yet cognitively able to process (e.g., first-year students really cannot use the *ATLA Religion Database* to find basic, background information about Martin Luther or a huge topic area such as 'communion'). It happens when faculty, in an attempt at introducing students to core journals in a field, require them to find more than one article on the same topic using only specific *journal titles* rather than helping their students learn how to effectively search the appropriate periodical index as a means of answering a research question. In some cases this onerous research scenario is further exacerbated when well-meaning faculty restrict their students to specific journal titles, a single topic idea and also a precise date range (e.g., use the following journal titles to locate three articles on 'management strategies' that were published in the last FIVE years). For the record, if a member of the teaching faculty really wants to see an academic librarian's head spin, they might also consider telling students that they may only use the *print* version of a particular journal. Each of these assignments demonstrates an immense 'disjuncture between the expectations of the faculty member as the expert researcher, and the capabilities of the undergraduate as the novice researcher' (Leckie, 1996: 203). Unfortunately, reference librarians are then left to deal with the inexperienced, often extremely frustrated new student standing before us.

As Todd Gilman notes in a recent article for *The Chronicle of Higher Education*, a number of studies show that even when new students demonstrate some technological acumen, these computer skills do not translate into information or research literacy (Gilman, 2009: para. 4). Additionally, today's libraries often seem incredibly complex to students who are new to campus. Even small academic libraries are now able to provide access to print and electronic resources of amazing scope and variety. If members of the teaching faculty do not anticipate their students' library inexperience or if they fail to provide adequate structure for and research guidance to these undergraduates, the results are usually exasperating for everyone involved. Students new to the research academy can suffer from library anxiety, utilize poor-quality sources of information and develop a serious dislike for (or fear of) future research-based assignments. Teaching faculty can feel frustrated by their first-year students who seem disinterested and unwilling to fully engage with the research process. These faculty members often end up dealing with students who noisily complain about being unable to find information, base their projects on superficial, poor-quality research or, worse, employ plagiarism in order to complete their assigned work.

Organization

This work has been divided into three main chapters. Chapter 1 introduces contemporary Millennial undergraduates and highlights a number of generational characteristics which seem to identify this distinctive group of new learners. This chapter also presents information literacy as a concept and goes on to explain why mastery of this set of proficiencies is vitally important for today's Millennial students. Finally, the book's first chapter emphasizes a number of potential strengths that collaborations between teaching faculty and academic librarians have and asserts the necessity for intentionally incorporating information literacy outcomes into first-year academic courses. Chapter 2 highlights a number of misconceptions about contemporary first-year students' research abilities and continues the argument for a strategic incorporation of information literacy outcomes into academic courses for novice researchers. Additionally, this chapter focuses on the need for taking a process-centered approach when asking these first-year students to undertake library research assignments. Chapter 2 closes with ideas for teaching faculty and academic librarians to consider as they negotiate concerns about information literacy education and its relationship to disciplinary course content. Chapter 3 puts forward some pedagogical approaches that teaching faculty might consider when looking for ways to incorporate information literacy into a first-year course. Suggestions for creating collaborative relationships, designing effective library assignments and approaching individual information literacy concepts are provided. Chapter 3 concludes with a discussion of the need for advancing information literacy educational programming beyond the first college year and provides examples of ways in which this crucial objective might be accomplished.

The Millennials go to the library: or do they?

Abstract: This chapter begins with a concise examination of several generational research studies which take today's Millennial students as their focus. The conclusions from several studies are then applied within the context of most first-year students' lack of academic research preparedness. This chapter also attempts to provide a definition for the oft-deliberated phrase *information literacy* as well as a rationale for why contemporary undergraduates urgently require greatly improved research proficiencies. Finally, this chapter focuses briefly on the value of collaboration between librarians and teaching faculty as a means of fostering information literacy work that is especially relevant and meaningful to contemporary undergraduates.

Key words: Millennials, first-year students, undergraduates, generational studies, information literacy, *Information Literacy Standards for Higher Education*, information competency, teaching faculty, librarians, collaboration(s).

Introducing the Millennials

The cohort of students currently entering American colleges and universities seems to have truly captured the imaginations of educators, researchers and pundits from a wide array of disciplines and backgrounds. The result has been an extensive body of literature which documents the unique cultural and social significance of this group of youngsters. A host of works have recently been written which document the major influences this generation has already exerted and will continue to have on the American economy, political arena, workplace, religious communities and other societal institutions (Alsop, 2008; Bauerlein, 2009; Buckingham, 2008; Howe and Strauss, 2007; Ito, 2010; Montgomery, 2007; Pletka, 2007; Tapscott, 2009, etc.). Alternately labeled 'Gen Y,' 'Generation Next,' the 'Digital Generation,' the 'Net Generation,' 'Echo Boomers,' or 'Millennials,' these students have had a tremendous effect on the organizations and individuals with whom they have come into contact, especially those of us working in higher education. While generalizations about entire groups (especially a group as diverse and seemingly eclectic as new college students) are always inexact, there is a general sense among academics that this group of students does require new ways of thinking about and utilizing a host of pedagogical strategies.

For some, the broad generational analyses of this particular group have resulted in decidedly optimistic portrayals. Neil Howe and William Strauss believe that the Millennials are 'recasting the youth mood in America' and that they are 'unlike any other youths in living memory' (2007: 7, 13). According to their recent book *Millennials Go to College*, Howe and Strauss consider this group 'more numerous, more affluent, better educated, and more ethnically diverse' than any prior generation. Indeed, for these two authors, Millennial students appear to have exceptionally 'positive social habits,' such as a belief in teamwork, achievement, modesty, and good conduct (2007: 13–14). According to John Palfrey and Urs Gasser's book *Born Digital*, this population is going to 'move markets and transform industries, education, and global politics' (2008: 7). Don Tapscott gushes that 'these empowered young people are beginning to transform every institution of modern life' (2009: 6). According to these authors and others, we in higher education have nothing to fear from our Millennial students. While their habits of learning, cultural interests and modes of socializing may be dramatically different from ours, their basic values remain in line with those of us who have other (older) generational memberships. As such, there is great promise in the suggestion that we might still productively engage with Millennial students (Ito et al., 2010: 342, 344).

Yet, other investigators question such overwhelmingly glowing generational descriptions, calling them 'hyperbolic idealizations' made by 'pro-technology' adults trying to construct this cohort as somehow 'exotic' (Herring, 2008: 76). Mark Bauerlein, an especially vocal digital detractor, argues that despite their extraordinary confidence in and use of technology, 'The twenty-first-century teen, connected and multitasked, autonomous yet peer-mindful, marks no great leap forward in human intelligence, global thinking, or "netizen"-ship' (2009: 201). Interestingly, even Larry Sanger, co-creator of the famously popular online site *Wikipedia*, is worried about this generation and the future of American education. Sanger strongly advocates for his version of a 'liberal education,' the kind that is built around an 'effortful, careful development of the individual mind' (2010: para. 45). He fears that without this type of didactic exertion, sources such as *Wikipedia* will be exploited by 'a society of drones, enculturated by hive minds, who are able to work together online but who are largely innocent of the texts and habits of study that encourage deep and independent thought' (para. 47). Sonia Livingstone, yet another Internet critic, adds further credence to Sanger's concerns. Livingstone writes that 'young people's Internet literacy does not yet match the headline image of the intrepid pioneer' (2008: 110). She believes this is mainly because the vast majority of young people have not developed the critical thinking skills necessary to vigilantly evaluate the resources they discover on the Internet. According to her 2008 focus group study, 'most children and young people' are 'ignorant of the motives behind the Web sites they were using' and most never bother to consider the question (2008: 109). As such, Livingstone maintains that while these youngsters' 'newfound online skills' may be 'justifiably trumpeted,' by the adults with whom they live and work, these skills are far from being above 'critical scrutiny' (102).

Authors such as Bauerlein, Sanger and Livingstone send a rather less encouraging message about today's undergraduate population. Instead of viewing them as 'the smartest generation ever,' these authors tend to believe the Millennials are becoming 'bound by the prejudices of [their] "digital tribe," ripe for manipulation by whoever has the firmest grip on [their] dialogue' (Tapscott, 2009: 30; Sanger, 2010: para. 47). According to this darker view, Millennial students are hopelessly enmeshed with the Internet and, as a result, they suffer academically. They are so plugged into online social networks that they pay little or no attention to real-life interactions. Their attempts at multitasking have disastrously harmful results, and they could not care less about the quality, reliability or accuracy of the information they find online and then use in their daily lives. These youngsters base any research they do solely on speed and ease of use. According to these less generous descriptions, present-day students are disengaged, prone to attention deficits and extremely difficult to teach using traditionally proven methods.

In reality, most Millennial students demonstrate a remarkably complex combination of characteristics which probably lands them somewhere in the middle of being the next greatest generation or the world's worst generation. As Ron Alsop notes, many 'educators and employers have found that [the Millennials] exhibit a number of contradictory attitudes and behaviors':

> 'It's all about me' might seem to be the mantra of these self-absorbed young people . . . But, many millennials . . . also demonstrate strong concern about social and environmental issues and tend to be active in community service. In another interesting twist, they want structure and clear direction in their work assignments, but they also expect flexibility to decide when and where they complete the tasks. And although they crave individual praise and recognition, they can also be terrific team players, whether in sports, the classroom or the workplace. (Alsop, 2008: 6)

Whether you believe that the outlook for today's Millennials is primarily positive, overly negative or somewhere in between, it is impossible to escape the fact that this generation of students is different if for no other reason than they are more plugged in than past generations have ever been. As Kathryn Montgomery notes in her book *Generation Digital*, 'Never before has a generation been so defined in the public mind by its relationship to technology' (2007: 2). Ask any educator about working with today's Millennial students and almost without a doubt the conversation will turn to the impact of the Internet, social networking, cell phones, electronic book readers or any of a number of popular technological gadgets on student learning.

Characteristics of this new generation

While it is beyond the scope of this book to examine in its entirety the wealth of Millennial research which currently exists, several well-recognized publications are worth highlighting for their careful generational portrayals. One such work, Palfrey and Gasser's *Born Digital: Understanding the First Generation of Digital Natives*, takes a slightly different approach than other generational studies. Early in the text, these authors indicate that there is an enormous and growing global technology divide among this generation. Therefore, rather than portray the 'digital natives' as an entirely homogeneous group, Palfrey and Gasser regard this faction as an extremely fortunate subset of their generational cohort (2008: 14). Having made this initial distinction, however, the authors go on to identify a number of overarching categories into which the members of this technologically privileged sub-group commonly fit. According to Palfrey and Gasser, today's tech-savvy young people are usually 'creators,' 'pirates,' 'aggressors,' 'innovators,' 'learners,' and/or 'activists' (2008: vii). Furthermore, while the authors understand that the digital natives are part of a much broader global generation, it is also clear that Palfrey and Gasser see many more modern commonalities among this highly networked group. For example, near the beginning of their book the authors reiterate the distinctiveness of today's young people.

> They study, work, write, and interact with each other in ways that are very different from the ways that you did growing up. They read blogs rather than newspapers. They often meet each other online before they meet in person. They probably don't even know what a library

card looks like, much less have one; and if they do, they've probably never used it. (2008: 2)

Beyond being perplexed by library cards, this group of ardent Internet users is, at its most basic level, 'part of a population born digital with different habits, attitudes, and beliefs' (289).

The view that today's Millennials are unquestionably different from previous school-age cohorts is shared by Bob Pletka, who, in his book *Educating the Net Generation*, agrees that this unique group of students has 'been nurtured by a world of digital technology, instant information, global communication, and individually customized environments' and that they are 'different from any previous generation' (2007: 21). Pletka goes on to assert that for these students, technology has been ingrained into all societal functions 'from relationships to commerce.' As a result, Pletka's net generation is 'comfortable multitasking' and has high expectations of their educational experiences, including 'experiential, dynamic, and cooperative activities facilitated through information and communication technologies' (21). These students are particularly non-responsive to passive learning environments and often do not hesitate to make their preference for experiential learning known.

Don Tapscott of the University of Toronto has written several noteworthy texts about information technology and its societal impact. According to his most recent monograph, *Grown Up Digital*, the Millennials demonstrate eight key characteristics which differentiate them from other generations:

They prize freedom and freedom of choice. They want to customize things, make them their own. They're natural collaborators, who enjoy a conversation, not a lecture. They'll scrutinize you and your organization. They insist on integrity. They want to have fun, even at work and at school. Speed is normal. Innovation is part of life. (2009: 6–7)

According to Tapscott, these students are 'smarter, quicker, and more tolerant of diversity' than any generation before. They engage politically because they care about civic participation and social justice. These students, says Tapscott, will forever change society and its organizations for the good (6). Similarly, Howe and Strauss's book describes seven 'core traits' of contemporary students. According to them, Millennial students are: 'special', 'sheltered', 'confident', 'team-oriented', 'conventional', 'pressured' and 'achieving'. Echoing Tapscott's effusive optimism, Howe and Strauss also believe that this generation is 'on track to becoming the smartest, best-educated [group of] young adults in US history' (2007: 59–60).

As noted earlier in this chapter, many of the familiar characteristics identified by previous authors and ostensibly demonstrated by Millennial students are extremely promising, and that may be a very good thing. Few and far between are the instructors who prefer teaching students who are *not* interactive, achieving, smart and socially aware. Even Bauerlein grudgingly admits that American teenagers can be 'energetic, ambitious, enterprising, and good' (2009: 10). Yet, when we take a closer look at the ways in which these lively students rely on technology (especially the Internet) to support their academic studies, it becomes clear, as Bauerlein goes on to say, that their 'talents and interests and money thrust them not into books and ideas and history and civics,' but into a very different and difficult place (10).

Within the field of library and information science (LIS), a great deal of time and effort has gone into investigating undergraduate students' attitudes about, knowledge of, and research abilities in libraries (Birmingham et al., 2008; Byerly et al., 2006; Caspers and Bernhisel, 2007; Connaway et al., 2008: 125–6; Kunkel et al., 1996; Weiler, 2004; etc.). While the results of this work have never been encouraging, it is especially disappointing to note that today's Millennial students continue to arrive on campuses with shockingly inadequate library research skills. As early as 1996, Gloria J. Leckie described the lack of research abilities among new students in her seminal journal article, 'Desperately Seeking Citations: Uncovering Faculty Assumptions about the Undergraduate Research Process.' Leckie's articulate (and rather lengthy) explanation of the research novice's incomplete and inefficient library process follows.

> Undergraduates, particularly those in the lower years, are exposed to certain disciplines for the first time. This exposure frequently consists of a textbook, reserve materials, and lectures. The students have no sense of who might be important in a particular field, and find it difficult to build and follow a citation trail. They do not have the benefit of knowing anyone who actually does research in the discipline [except their professor] and so do not have a notion of something as intangible as the informal scholarly network. They have never attended a scholarly conference. Because of their level of cognitive development, ambiguity and non-linearity may be quite threatening. *They do not think in terms of an information-seeking strategy, but rather in terms of a coping strategy.* Research is conceptualized as a fuzzy library-based activity which is required of them to complete their coursework. (Leckie, 1996: 202–3, emphasis added)

Though it was written some fifteen years ago, Leckie's piece is as relevant today as it was then. In her analysis of young college students' poor library performance, she places the responsibility for their weak research skills where it belongs. Leckie does not blame students or the research tools they try to use. Rather, she believes that the real issue is a disconnect which exists between what teaching faculty assume about their new undergraduates' research skills and the amount of actual experience these students have had in academic libraries, with complex academic disciplines and writing college-level papers.

More recently, William Badke has furthered this argument when he writes that 'those in secondary school have almost no understanding of library systems, *are averse to using libraries* and are inept when they finally do access a catalog or database' (2005: 48, emphasis added). In her review of the current literature, Mary Ann Fitzgerald adds that even though today's undergraduates may 'have grown up with the Internet, they have not improved in their level of sophistication in assessing the quality of online resources' (2004: 22). She goes on to state that most contemporary students 'have [a] poor understanding of many types of basic and authoritative reference resources' and 'are ill-prepared to perform complex database searches' (21). Caroline Geck (2006) explains that indeed, there is a fundamental lack of understanding about the basic organizational structure of information which goes beyond confusion about academic libraries. Geck observes that today's technologically proficient youngsters do not have 'a deep understanding of the inner workings of the Internet or how commercial search engines rank results.' As a result these students flounder, spending 'exorbitant amounts of time browsing' through items that are often completely irrelevant to their assignments (2006: 20). Palfrey and Gasser also warn that 'the majority of the population born digital doesn't perceive quality of information as an important issue' (2008: 161). As most teaching faculty and academic librarians already know, the students entering our colleges and universities today may well be a generation of technologically savvy, well-connected computer connoisseurs. But as Todd Gilman comments in his recent article in *The Chronicle of Higher Education*, these undergraduates are simply not research-literate and there is a profound difference between the two (2009: para. 4).

What is information literacy and do contemporary undergraduates really need it?

In order to answer either of these questions, a bit of background about the library profession's information literacy movement (formerly known as bibliographic instruction) may be helpful. On January 10th, 1989, members of the American Library Association's (ALA) Presidential Committee on Information Literacy submitted their influential *Final Report* in which they began what has been a lengthy process of calling attention to the need for greater emphasis on information literacy in the United States (ALA, 1989). This committee was especially concerned about the speed at which the information age was racing across the nation. They also recognized that as this movement quickly advanced, it added layer upon layer of economic, societal and cultural complexities onto a global community that was increasingly dependent upon information and technology work. According to committee members, in order to successfully deal with this new, high-speed world, people need more than just a knowledge base, they also need techniques for exploring it, connecting it to other knowledge bases, and making practical use of it. In other words, the landscape upon which we used to stand has been transformed, and we are being forced to establish a new foundation called information literacy. (ALA, 1989: para. 38)

More than twenty years later, the perspective of most professional librarians has changed little. Consequently, the short answers to what information literacy is, and whether or not contemporary undergraduates really need it or not, likely go something like this: information literacy is a set of skills which allow people to 'recognize when information is needed and have the ability to locate, evaluate, and use effectively the needed information' (ALA, 1989: para. 5). And yes, based on years of experience working with undergraduates in classrooms and at reference desks across the country, modern-day students of all ages continue to be in desperate need of developing these proficiencies. As the introduction to the 2000 Association of College and Research Libraries' (ACRL) seminal *Information Literacy Competency Standards for Higher Education* more eloquently points out, 'As students progress through their undergraduate years and graduate programs, they need to have repeated opportunities for seeking, evaluating, and managing information gathered from multiple sources and discipline-specific research methods' (ACRL, 2000: 5). Simply stated, practice makes perfect.

Expecting students to develop their research skills as undergraduates is really nothing new. Students of any age have always benefited academically from being able to recognize, understand, evaluate and effectively use information. In many ways, teaching faculty from all disciplines have done information literacy for years. Every time a faculty member works with a student to negotiate an interesting, manageable paper topic, or offers students guidance about the expectations for information source quality, or even helps a student manage their way through the appropriate disciplinary citation style format, students have the opportunity to practice and demonstrate information literacy competencies. Yet, it is extremely important to remember that no matter how computer-savvy these students appear, making value judgments about online, electronically available resources is not a skill young people innately possess (Palfrey and Gasser, 2008: 167). Without explicit instruction about and regular practice with contemporary information technologies, or efficient research strategies and specific evaluative techniques, students will continue to use highly questionable approaches to complete their academic work.

> Adolescents with a lot of Web experience often base their evaluations of online information on personal preferences . . . Visual aspects, such as personal color and design preferences, rank among the top evaluation criteria for judging the depth of online information, often more than, for instance, the sources cited. Further, information quality tends to be equated with information quantity. (Palfrey and Gasser, 2008: 167)

New undergraduates need to repeatedly apply their nascent research and evaluation skills to academic assignments which require them to critically analyze, synthesize and create something new with the information they find. They also need librarians and teaching faculty to guide them through, and to provide meaningful feedback on, their research processes. This is yet another reason ALA's early call for making information literacy a 'central, not a peripheral, concern,' particularly in schools and other educational institutions has become increasingly more crucial as time goes by (ALA, 1989: para. 32).

Academic librarians know that members of our profession have long been discussing, studying and publishing what we know about teaching library tools and complex search methods to novice researchers (Lorenzen, 2001). Unfortunately for the discipline, many of the scholarly publications examining this long-established work are not on the radar of most teaching faculty at colleges and universities (Birmingham et al., 2008: 7–9; Fister, 1995). For librarians this means that their closest educational allies, the very people who are best situated to advocate for and assess undergraduates' information literacy competencies, may not know how to best challenge and support students who are new to campus and who often have little if any aptitude for library research. This has also meant that a great deal of confusion about the concept of 'information literacy' remains among members of the academy, some of whom are suspicious that this new expression signals yet another ephemeral pedagogical fad.

A number of attempts have been made to further clarify what it is that members of the library profession mean when using the phrase information literacy (Wilson, 2004). Perhaps the most ambitious and ultimately controversial effort was made in January, 2000. At this time members of ACRL's Board of Directors approved the *Information Literacy Competency Standards for Higher Education*. In addition to offering a lengthy list of highly structured standards, performance indicators and outcomes, this document defined information literacy as follows:

> Information literacy forms the basis for lifelong learning. It is common to all disciplines, to all learning

environments, and to all levels of education. It enables learners to master content and extend their investigations, become more self-directed, and assume greater control over their own learning. An information literate individual is able to:

- Determine the extent of information needed
- Access the needed information effectively and efficiently
- Evaluate information and its sources critically
- Incorporate selected information into one's knowledge base
- Use information effectively to accomplish a specific purpose
- Understand the economic, legal, and social issues surrounding the use of information, and access and use information ethically and legally. (ACRL, 2000: para. 7–8)

Today, the *Standard*s are used in a variety of contexts. Together, librarians and teaching faculty have modified and used them as a basis for formulating information literacy outcomes which meet the requirements of their general education curricula. Some librarians have worked with the members of individual departments within their colleges and universities to develop disciplinary-based information literacy outcomes for their majors and/or minors. The *Standards* have also been used by countless academic librarians as a means of simply getting the information literacy conversation started on their campuses.

While it is rare that librarians and teaching faculty agree upon all facets of the *Standards*, this set of performance indicators remains a valuable tool for exploring the complex concept that is information literacy. Information literacy has far-reaching consequences for modern-day Millennials. For those students who graduate without being information literate will certainly have a difficult road ahead once they no longer have their professors, mentors or academic librarians guiding them through today's rapidly expanding information landscape.

Assessing the quality of information is a difficult task for anyone. It requires that various factors be taken into account, ranging from previous bits of knowledge to contextual information. And the task of making quality judgments gets cognitively more demanding as the complexity of the information increases. Where there is interplay among a lot of factual elements, for instance, or in situations where normative judgments are required, deliberate quality assessments become so complicated that people often avoid them altogether (Palfrey and Gasser, 2008: 165).

Academic librarians have watched patrons base their information-gathering strategies on pure expediency for years. The difference today is that expediency often comes down to a few seconds or a single computer screen hurriedly pulled up on a student's laptop, rather than a research process that may, in the past, have actually required multiple hours spent in the physical library building. Because Millennials have had little reason to cultivate persistence or tenacity, the idea of applying high-quality information literacy techniques does not even occur to them. This is yet another of the many reasons why ACRL's *Standards* are generally recognized (at the very least in spirit) at most contemporary academic libraries in the United States.

This is not to say that information literacy as a concept no longer generates discussion among librarians and academics or that its definition has ever really been static. Once ACRL's document became public, the already lively debate over how to further define and clarify the phrase has continued to develop (Elmborg, 2006; Levitov, 2004; Orme, 2008; Owusu-Ansah, 2003; Swanson, 2006). As modern information technology continues to transform itself, authors persist in recasting, rephrasing and/or restating what they believe it means to be information literate. Livingstone remarks that today 'the notion of information literacy has been developed to encompass the competencies required to design and use complex digital systems for the representation and distribution of information' (2008: 107).

For example, in a recent book chapter Loanne Snavely provides yet another contemporary interpretation of what it means to be information literate.

> For an individual to be prepared for independent inquiry, whether as a matter of individual curiosity or for a community or work-related need, having the skills and strategies for acquiring information on a new topic or in a new field, knowing how to formulate the questions to be answered, selecting appropriate resources and databases to search, conducting effective and efficient searches, and evaluating the appropriateness of the information are all part of the underpinnings of learning to learn. The subsequent tasks of reading, comprehending, analyzing, synthesizing, and integrating new knowledge into what is already known, and using that to create new knowledge and meaning, is the true power of being information literate. (Snavely, 2008: 36)

While less formal in tone than ACRL's original document, Snavely's adaptation continues to emphasize the same key concepts included in the originally published *Standards*. Both then and now information literacy's main focus continues to be on educating young people to become lifelong learners, an enterprise teaching faculty and librarians have continually, though not always collaboratively, taken on.

Attitudinal shifts: addressing truculence in the faculty lounge

In August of 2008, Daphnée Rentfrow, a PhD in Comparative Literature and (at the time) a current student in library school at the University of Illinois, Urbana-Champaign was asked to contribute a chapter to the Council on Library and Information Resources report, *No Brief Candle: Reconceiving Research Libraries for the 21st Century*. In it, Rentfrow drew on her own experience as a professor and a scholar to share her concerns about what she saw as a major challenge facing college and university libraries across the country. Her focus was on the relationships (or lack thereof) between librarians and teaching faculty at these institutions. Rentfrow wrote that teaching faculty

> are the single greatest challenge facing the modern research and academic library. Without faculty support and understanding and without their regular collaboration with librarians, the research library will not survive. It may remain as an interesting museum piece or storage facility, but it will no longer be the heart of the institution. (Rentfrow, 2008: 60)

Rentfrow went on to write that, regrettably, even though academic librarians have long been managing 'seismic changes' across the entire profession, not to mention identifying a myriad of 'ways in which the profession can and should be intimately involved with advanced research and undergraduate education,' these upheavals in the profession seem not to have 'changed how scholars think of the library' (60). As a faculty member from my own institution unhappily notes, 'In my humble opinion, professors often see the library/librarians as a service to use, the same as the cafeteria or post office' (Twomey, 2010). After years of managing complex, constantly changing information technologies and patiently advocating for information literacy, this is a terribly difficult message for most academic librarians. Yet as disappointing as it is, Rentfrow's message is not entirely unexpected, as a number of studies exist which place librarians and teaching faculty at odds with one another (Badke, 2005; Given and Julien, 2005; Hardesty, 1995; McGuinness, 2006). Whether it is an impenetrable faculty culture, a sense of defensiveness on the part of librarians, or, what is more likely, a complicated mixture of issues far beyond the scope of this book, the fact is that librarians and teaching faculty have not always communicated well with one another. Sadly, the result of this discontinuity has likely affected our students more than it has either of the two parties vying for influence.

Happily, there are indications that past attitudes and the resultant less-than-cooperative work environment may be evolving. Today, the prospects for partnering with one another are opening up on many college and university campuses. Collaborations between teaching faculty and librarians are increasingly doing well at 'teaching institutions which recognize that faculty members have expertise in their subject discipline and that librarians have expertise that is conceptual, process-oriented, and interdisciplinary' (Rockman, 2004a: 241). Whether or not a previously acrimonious atmosphere surrounded librarians and faculty at an institution should no longer deter the collaborative impulse. After all, information technologies continue to evolve at a frightening pace, institutional accountability requirements are only getting more stringent and it is clear that neither librarians nor teaching faculty can afford to go it alone when it comes to ensuring their students are prepared to be critical thinkers and lifelong learners upon graduation.

Consequently, while it may be true that 'librarians seldom operate from a position of strength in their relationships with the faculty,' it is also true that teaching faculty 'are having as much trouble as non-academics keeping up with the information explosion, including, of course, learning new library research skills' (Hardesty, 1995: para. 109; Jenkins, 2005: 23). Bundy restates this view when he remarks that because of the increasingly complex nature of today's knowledge-based information universe, 'curricula, pedagogy and assessment can no longer be the sole province of individual academic teachers' (2004: 2). He therefore advocates for dramatically changing the instructional nature at institutions of higher education, so much so that teaching becomes an entirely 'disaggregated team effort' (2). While Bundy's ambitious vision may be years away, it would nevertheless be wise for those of us who work at institutions of higher education to recognize that when it comes to dealing with the considerable information literacy needs of our students, we need one another now more than ever.

According to Susan Carol Curzon, 'faculty and librarians together can make a formidable team' (2004: 29). In her chapter 'Developing Faculty–Librarian Partnerships for Information Literacy,' Curzon begins by identifying the key strengths that librarians and teaching faculty can take advantage of when working together to advance information literacy skills across their campuses.

> The cornerstone of an information literacy program that flourishes and endures on a campus is the powerful partnership between faculty and librarians. Faculty have governance of the curriculum, a steady influence on students, and mastery of their discipline. Librarians have exceptional information research skills, knowledge

> of student searching behavior, and a commitment to the
> importance of information literacy. (Curzon, 2004: 29)

By working together, teaching faculty and librarians provide a wealth of expertise (both disciplinary and research-based), a variety of useful investigative strategies, and the kind of valuable support most novice researchers need to successfully complete their academic work. As one study recently discovered, although most young teenagers 'benefit from a consistent message and a consistent approach to information literacy,' they also need 'opportunities to explore a variety of information strategies with the support of mediating professionals, adults, and peers' (Meyers, Fisher and Marcoux, 2009: 335). Working together further ensures that new Millennial students receive consistent, reliable messages about their campus library (or libraries) as well as lots of practice with the research tools that are most appropriate to a first-year student's information needs. Such teamwork also provides new undergraduates with valuable opportunities to interact with veteran research professionals, experience applying a variety of valuable information research strategies, and undertake course-based research assignments that are innovative, engaging and meaningful.

Today, collaborations between librarians and teaching faculty take many forms (Rockman, 2004c: 47). In fact, studies show that 'close collaboration between librarians and faculty members is a hallmark of successful IL (information literacy) programs' (Malone and Videon, 2007: 59). Though it may take some time to create these effective partnerships, successful collaborations often begin when a member or members of the teaching faculty and academic librarians recognize their shared concern for undergraduate research and student success. Once this initial commonality is acknowledged, a successful collaboration can then be nurtured through direct communication, careful content negotiation and scrupulous planning. This shared work can create rewarding academic partnerships that blossom into programmatic approaches which are particularly helpful to students new to the academic library and to the rigors of scholarly research:

> Many undergraduate libraries have reached out to secondary schools to help prepare students for the academic transition to the college and university setting as well as become actively involved with freshman seminar and first-year learning programs on their campuses. These programs are often linked with other college or university programs (such as learning communities) and are intended to help students successfully meet the academic standards of college. (Rockman, 2004c: 51).

Though many campuses in the United States have reached a certain level of programmatic collaboration between the teaching faculty and those librarians who mainly work with first-year students, the extent to which information literacy competencies have become key, measurable outcomes for even these undergraduates continues to vary greatly by institution. This variance leaves many academic librarians in the position of continually pursuing further faculty support in recognition of the fact that librarians simply 'cannot go it alone' (Curzon, 2004: 30). Curzon goes on to say that without 'a partnership with and a base of support from the faculty' academic librarians 'who are committed to a goal of student mastery of information literacy' have an impossible task (30).

In my own experience, one of the impediments to close collaborative work has been a situation where teaching faculty continue to feel unsure about what it is exactly that their academic librarian colleagues can or will actually *do* for professors or for their students. Often when I visit with a new member of the teaching faculty or even those individuals who may not have had an opportunity to work with first-year students for some time, these professors are surprised at the level to which integrating information literacy competencies has become pedagogically essential.

> When IL (information literacy) is integrated within the first-year curriculum, the program reaches more students and offers them higher quality instruction. Once classroom faculty members from numerous disciplines have integrated IL concepts in their courses, librarians can play a reinforcing role by assisting with the design of assignments and providing supplementary exercises, materials, and database demonstrations. (Malone and Videon, 2007: 59)

The truth is that today, most successful collaborations begin with librarians. Academic librarians often start by 'articulating a basic definition of what they need to do and then working closely with classroom faculty members to be sure the faculty understand the various aspects of information literacy' (Malone and Videon, 2007: 51). Unfortunately, according to Curzon, this approach can also lead to trouble in the future. She warns that information literacy programs often fail because 'they are parochial and eventually come to be seen as only a library effort' (Curzon, 2004: 35). In Curzon's mind,

> The information literacy program should be introduced as an enterprise-wide solution to an enterprise-wide problem. To catch the attention of faculty and academic

administrators, information literacy must be part of the academic effort rather than just a toolbox of skills that students learn in order to use the library. (35)

How, then, might members of the teaching faculty further influence information literacy programming and ensure a successful collaborative relationship with their academic librarians? The flippant (yet effective) answer is to simply find an academic librarian, any academic librarian, and ASK. The vast majority of academic librarians are eager to support their teaching faculty at *any stage* of course and/or assignment preparation. In fact, the earlier academic librarians are brought into a course the more effective the collaboration is likely to be.

Working with an academic librarian provides a number of advantages. By visiting with a librarian well in advance of prepping a course, professors ensure several things. First, getting the class on the radar of an academic librarian will allow these information professionals to provide collection development and acquisitions support, further ensuring that the library's collection contains current, relevant, interesting sources that are directly applicable to the course's content. Librarians at many institutions even notify faculty when a topical new DVD, video or book arrives and is ready for check-out. Second, teaching faculty who develop their syllabi in collaboration with an academic librarian allow these research experts to share their valuable counsel on the kinds of research competencies undergraduates are likely to have or not have. Such insights can definitely make a positive impact on the success of a required research project or, at a minimum, influence how the project might be most effectively scaffolded across a course. As Curzon advises, 'librarians see the often messy process of students doing information research. The process affects the outcome. If faculty are not happy with the quality of papers and other assignments turned in, they may want to influence the process of information research' (2004: 33). When considering students' likely research processes in cooperation with an academic librarian, course planning becomes proactive rather than reactive to typical undergraduate library research challenges. Academic librarians can suggest ways of working together so that novice researchers are not only challenged by the library work they do but appropriately supported as well. Finally, most academic librarians today are enthusiastic class presenters. Library professionals attend entire conferences, read books and cruise full journal issues focused on contemporary pedagogical strategies and best teaching practices. While certainly there are librarians who are more skilled in the classroom than others, at the very least, asking an academic librarian about the possibility of scheduling a library session should get you a recommendation for a member of the library staff who will be available and qualified to help.

There is little debate that members of the faculty are, by far, an academic librarian's most valuable allies. According to Jenkins, there is 'no other group' with 'a greater influence over the student body and its use of the library' (2005: 35). Whether librarians have clearly and actively articulated this or not on some college campuses may be debatable, yet, as Raymond McInnis maintains, *most* academic librarians are acutely aware that:

> More than any other factor, the value the classroom instructor attaches to library research determines the students' interest in and use of library materials. Instructors give direction and motivation to students as to how library materials are to be used in meeting course requirements. Their influence is most often the

difference between a perfunctory use of materials and dedicated examination of the rich store of . . . literature typically available in most college libraries. (McInnis, 1978: 3)

If librarians at colleges and universities want undergraduates to use library resources, we must have teaching faculty who understand and support the work we do and who also make library research a critical course component. When members of the teaching faculty are reluctant to utilize their librarian colleagues' expertise, library staff and, most importantly, our shared undergraduate students, are often left in dire straits. As William Miller and Steven Bell observe, 'No librarian, no matter how gifted an instructor, can squeeze a round peg of information literacy into some square hole in the student's mind . . . if the [library] instruction lacks centrality to course content, it's likely to fail' (2005: para. 13). For all of the unique aspects and responsibilities of our professional work, librarians and teaching faculty must (at a minimum) communicate more effectively. The more knowledge we share with one another about the undergraduate research process, research-based course assignments, disciplinary inquiry and the value of information literacy to lifelong learning, the more likely it is that students will begin to see the value of research competencies not only in their educational futures, but to their personal lives as well. Those of us working at institutions of higher education share the common purpose of helping students learn to be lifelong, effective and efficient information consumers. As Jenkins remarks, 'librarians are teachers at heart,' and so this partnership makes especially good sense (2005: 77).

As our lightning-paced global information landscape continues to expand, librarians and teaching faculty are going to be increasingly hard-pressed *not* to form partnerships for the benefit of our mainly untaught undergraduate researchers. A recent article published in *The Economist* reveals the increasing importance information literacy will have for the Millennials well beyond their college years. This piece estimates that the amount of online information or data currently being created 'increases tenfold every five years' (*Economist* 2010: para. 12). The article goes on to project that 'by 2013 the amount of traffic flowing over the Internet annually will reach 667 exabytes' (para. 12). Hal Varian, Google's chief economist, worries that a major dilemma has resulted from such large amounts of data becoming so easily accessible. He believes the competency that is most 'scarce is the ability to extract wisdom from' this enormous amount of data (para. 9). Alex Szalay, an astrophysicist from Johns Hopkins University agrees, 'How to make sense of all these data? People should be worried about how we train the next generation, not just of scientists, but people in government and industry' (para. 5). There really is no avoiding the fact that teaching faculty and academic librarians at institutions of higher education are becoming increasingly responsible for this training. As Rockman notes, research from within the LIS field makes it quite clear that 'students are not picking up information literacy skills on their own' (2004b: 16). Luckily, as Curzon understands it, 'faculty want their students to be successful throughout life [and] they . . . appreciate that students who graduate with information literacy skills can keep learning throughout life and keep contributing to their profession and to society' (2004: 33). Fortunately, this underlying philosophy is one that academic librarians share and regularly promote, providing the impulse for collaborative work between these two groups yet another important common place from where to begin.

Preparing Millennials to enter a knowledge-based civilization that is already clogged with vast amounts of disorganized and/or unreliable data is a complex, labor-intensive prospect. Yet, by working together to combine our pedagogical strengths and our disciplinary expertise, collaborations between teaching faculty and academic librarians can ensure that undergraduate students have a variety of positive learning experiences with a range of research strategies and information technologies. Given lots of practice and numerous opportunities to apply newfound information competencies, students can leave colleges and universities having gained an informed understanding of the many ways in which today's data is created, organized and produced.

> With information literacy skills a student's academic life is deeply enriched, their academic achievement is enabled, and their capacity for lifelong learning is enhanced. When our students have mastery of information literacy, librarians and faculty have done their job as educators. Information literacy is an important cause. (Curzon, 2004: 44)

Most academic librarians today see information literacy as more than an 'important cause.' According to the Association of American Colleges and Universities' (AAC&U) 2002 report, *Greater Expectations: A New Vision for Learning as a Nation Goes to College*, 'The best undergraduate education for the twenty-first century will be based on a liberal education that produces an individual who is intentional about learning and life, empowered, informed and responsible' (AAC&U, 2002: 25). It seems impossible for *any* educational experience to generate such ambitious traits in its undergraduates without making information literacy an integral curricular component. Therefore, information literacy is not just an important cause, it is an essential one.

Conclusion

In their chapter devoted to information quality, Palfrey and Gasser point out that 'The ability to make quality judgments about information on the Internet is not an innate skill' (2008: 167). Though many Millennial first-year students arrive at college having spent an extraordinary amount of time accumulating, sharing and playing with digital technologies, they do *not* arrive having spent much, if any, time applying reasoning, problem-solving or critical thinking skills to this technology use. These same highly-connected students will have serious difficulties when asked to complete even seemingly simple library research assignments. Not because they do not know enough about computer technology or surfing the Internet, but because there is a tremendous difference between using the latest electronic gadgets with ease and effectively using the *information* that is accessible through these gadgets. Teaching faculty and academic librarians must work together for the benefit of our newest students in an environment such as this because

> The world of information is large and complex. There are no easy answers to providing simplified searching to the wealth of electronic information resources produced by a wide range of publishers using different structures and vocabularies. Students may perceive that librarians have developed systems that are complex and make sense to informational professionals but are too difficult to use without being an expert. (Lippincott, 2005: 13.4)

Predictably, most new students today do not eagerly embrace academic libraries. This is nothing new. Undergraduates have always needed a great deal of library support, especially those in their first year of college. What *is* dramatically different, however, is the amount of information from around the world that is currently accessible through academic libraries and the Internet. Today's research tools far exceed what even our most engaged students might imagine. Therefore, it is imperative that these students not be allowed to opt out of using their campus libraries simply because they have preconceived notions about libraries, academic librarians or even what constitutes acceptable college-level research. If we are going to successfully prepare young people to be thoughtful and informed lifelong learners, they must be taught how to focus on information content rather than get distracted by stereotypes and gadgetry.

I was reminded of the importance of this task during a recent class session I did for a group of first- and second-year students. I asked the group to break into pairs so that they might examine and report on a number of course-related library sources that I had gathered for them. Each pair was to explore their assigned source and to identify the type of information it provided, figure out how it worked and, finally, tell their classmates whether or not they recommended using it. After spending 15 minutes or so examining the six print volumes of the *Encyclopedia of Latin American History and Culture*, one team of students decided that they would hesitatingly recommend it because it did contain exactly the kind of information they needed (the course was an introduction to Latin American studies). However, they also went on to say, they would NOT recommend it because their classmates would have to walk 'all the way over to the library' to get it (our campus is extremely small) and also because it was 'too heavy.' Eliminating an outstanding academic information source based on its heft is the kind of evaluative decision I see first-year students make all the time and, as Bauerlein writes, 'It isn't funny anymore' (2009: 234).

2

Information literacy in the context of the first year

Abstract: This chapter continues the dialog about the need for and increasing value of information literacy among first-year undergraduate students. It also facilitates serious consideration of the academic library's important educational purpose and its place as a true center for learning. Ultimately, Chapter 2 is meant to encourage a sustained conversation and greater collaborative work between teaching faculty and the academic librarians with whom they work.

Key words: novice researchers, first-year students, new undergraduates, Millennials, dependent learners, information literacy, information competency, evaluation, critical thinking, library research, technology use, research process, Internet, Information Search Process, ISP, teachable moment(s), information literacy programs, library assignment(s), student attitudes, point-of-need, course content.

Introduction

In the spring of 1988 Mary W. George, who was at that time Head of the General and Humanities Division at Princeton University, published a library aptitude 'wish list' for first-year students (George, 1988: 189). Among the eleven competencies she included were a number of pragmatic, lower-order, library use skills such as: having a rudimentary understanding of basic database and catalog searching; knowing what to expect of a library's 'resources, services, policies, and procedures;' and realizing the 'importance of accurate citations and a research log.' However, also included in George's list were several higher-order increasingly advanced research concepts. She opined that first-year students ought to: know how to ask 'fruitful questions;' differentiate between 'knowledge, information and opinion;' understand that research is a 'process of planned inquiry;' recognize the 'logic of discovery;' and be able to effectively evaluate, select and use relevant, reliable information sources (189). Because George's enumerated list was published without further contextual commentary, it is unclear if she realistically hoped students would arrive at her institution having already mastered each of these skills or if she believed her list might also serve as a type of outcomes document for students completing their first college year. What is clear, however, is that this particular academic librarian had high expectations of her newest undergraduates' research capabilities.

George's opinion piece is worth noting for several reasons. First among them is that her list functions as an excellent example of one academic librarian's attempt to advance library research instruction beyond what was at the time more commonly known as bibliographic instruction or BI. During the period George's list was published, bibliographic instruction was often focused on lower-order, procedurally-based library skills such as learning how to locate books in a library building or how to operate a specific research tool. Yet, George was pressing teaching faculty and librarians to provide the kind of library instruction that would prepare their first-year students to go far beyond merely being able to find scads of information by performing basic searches in a library catalog, electronic database or on the Internet. While she understood that mastering routine, skills-based strategies for doing library research would be a necessary *start* for newly minted first-year students, she also knew that turning them loose amid access to overwhelming amounts of information would not be structured enough nor supportive enough for students who were new to the expectations for college-level academic research. Accordingly, George's list intentionally included several increasingly complex, higher-order thinking proficiencies which focused attention on the multifaceted research challenges faced by new learners.

Mastery of advanced critical thinking competencies, such as those required of the information literate, has also been championed by a range of present-day authorities and futurists. The AAC&U's *Greater Expectations* report mentions a serious need for students to attain 'mental agility' as well as 'intellectual power' (AAC&U, 2002: 24). This report goes on to say that such critical judgment is more important than ever for contemporary students, and it ultimately calls for college graduates who are 'nimble thinkers and creative problem solvers' (24). Tapscott readily agrees, writing that today's undergraduates must be able to 'think creatively, critically, and collaboratively' as well as 'master the "basics" and excel in reading, math, science, and *information literacy* in order to 'respond to opportunities and challenges with speed, agility, and innovation' (2009: 127, [emphasis added],'). Patricia Senn Breivik reiterates this sentiment and goes on to suggest that students 'must be taught critical thinking skills that will help them determine when and where to find information and then how to identify, access, evaluate and effectively use that information' (Breivik, 2005: 22).

In a keynote address delivered in 2004, Christine Bruce demonstrates a similarly ardent view of the value information literacy competency provides undergraduates new to the academy. She remarks that the authentic 'significance of information literacy education lies in its potential to encourage deep, rather than surface learning, and in its potential to transform dependent learners into independent, self-directed, lifelong learners' (Bruce, 2004: para. 18). Sadly, as early as 1994 Hardesty had already observed that 'many classroom faculty members have never had occasion to think about the library as a major educational resource for undergraduate students' (Hardesty, 2007: xxiv). This lack of intentional consideration for or clear articulation of institutionally supported information literacy outcomes continues to be an especially challenging and regrettable curricular issue at many contemporary colleges and universities. As Palfrey and Gasser reiterate, even in today's extremely wired environment, the 'ability to separate credible information from less credible information' remains 'rarely addressed' by most academic curricula (2008: 181).

Thus, the chapter that follows seeks to begin a dialogue about the serious need for and increasing value of information literacy, particularly among first-year students. This chapter aims also to facilitate serious consideration of the academic library's educational purpose and its place as a center of the 'learning enterprise' for first-year students and the faculty who instruct them (Bennett, 2009: 194). Ultimately, Chapter 2 is meant to encourage sustained conversation and collaborative work between teaching faculty and academic librarians as together we make our way through the varied and thorny issues involved in navigating today's complicated, fast-paced, information-driven world. Such continuous exchanges can be especially helpful and enlivening for those of us who care deeply for our first-year students. Working together, faculty and librarians can actively contribute to the advancement of these students' academic success, increase their depth of intellectual development and encourage their progress toward attaining a number of valuable lifelong learning proficiencies.

A brief note about what this chapter does *not* do. This chapter does not engage in the debates surrounding questions of *how* information literacy competencies should be integrated into specific academic curricula. The author does not presume to have answers for questions concerning whether or not information literacy outcomes are best situated among general education requirements, across an entire curriculum, taught as the focus of stand-alone, credit-bearing courses or simply integrated broadly into individual courses and/or majors. These larger, programmatic discussions are left for others to take up. Rather, this text proceeds on the assumption that information literacy competencies should be an essential part of any first-year college or university student's educational experience. How those competencies become present within the curricula of unique schools of higher education remains a task for those individual faculty, librarians and their institutional leaders to work out.

Attending to novice researchers

How do you know if you are working with a novice library researcher? Academic librarians and teaching faculty alike will recognize signs such as these:

- The student is obviously anxious and nervously asks elementary questions that indicate he or she has very little experience generating effective search strategies, working with library information tools or writing researched papers.

- The student reports that she or he has been searching for a very long time and that the library has absolutely nothing on his or her topic idea.

- The student is unable to accurately paraphrase (and often has not brought along a copy of) the assignment and can therefore only give a vague description of the information he or she *thinks* is required (e.g., 'I need to find something about the environment.').

- Alternately, the student may sheepishly thrust a copy of her or his assignment at a reference librarian, assuming that this librarian will: a) immediately and correctly interpret the assignment without the benefit of course participation; b) instantly know which library research tool(s) or information resource(s) the instructor expects students to use in order to properly complete the project; and c) quickly and easily reel off the 'answer' to the assignment.

- The student is especially impatient and clearly unprepared to spend any length of time actually working on her or his project. These students frequently glance at their watches, chat with passing friends, text or even take cell-phone calls during library reference interviews. Often, these are the students who have not left themselves enough time to conduct meaningful research explorations of any kind. Such students have no comprehension of the notion that research is a protracted, recursive and reflective process.

This last scenario in particular seems to have become especially prevalent among today's wired teenagers. According to Carol Kuhlthau, Jannica Heinström and Ross Todd, the Internet has fundamentally altered students' attitudes about the research process by raising their expectations for finding information 'quickly and without effort and where choice of topic is guided by an estimate of easy availability' (2008: para. 5). Their article goes on to say that new undergraduates commonly ignore the earliest and most important research step, the 'preliminary, exploratory searching and focus formulation' phase. First-year students in particular regularly charge ahead with 'information collection for their final product,' without bothering to gain any 'background knowledge [or] formulating [the] essential questions that [will] drive and direct their information seeking' (para. 10). This detrimental habit means that to most first-year students effective research is mainly trouble-free and, above all else, *fast*.

An even more granular exploration of the speed equals quality phenomenon is described by Vicki Tolar Burton and her colleague Scott A. Chadwick. These authors found that students ranked their top three evaluative criteria for Internet source selection as, ' "source is easy to understand," "source is easy to find," and "source is available" ' (2000: 321). Additionally, students identified the same three criteria as being among the five most important measures for selecting library resources as well, 'indicating that accessibility – both physical and cognitive – is primary for students' (321). As if this proclivity for valuing the speed and convenience of research information over central criteria, such as relevance, significance, trustworthiness, timeliness, etc., is not an intractable enough misconception among Millennials, there is also evidence that only about a third of these incoming students meet their professors' expectations for reading comprehension during their first undergraduate year (ACT, 2009: 25–6). Therefore, not only will new undergraduates make many ill-informed choices as they gather information sources to complete college-level projects, even if these novice researchers do manage to run across a reliable academic resource (no matter *what* the format), a significant number may disregard it based solely on their inability to read and understand it.

For these and other reasons too numerous to enumerate here, first-year students are considered an institution's most dependent learners. Indeed, Robert Leamnson describes them as presenting 'the greatest challenge to college and university teachers' everywhere (2003: 2). Anyone who has spent time trying to instruct this capricious cohort likely understands all too well that first-year students require extraordinary patience, plentiful practice and significant amounts of gentle pushing. As Leamnson points out, first-year students already come to higher education having developed a number of unique preconceptions about learning. This means that it is especially important for anyone involved in their education to 'consider and reflect, not only on what they teach, but how they teach' it (3). For example, many first-year students come to institutions already resistant to certain instructional forms. Having been 'nurtured in an environment where digital information technologies personalize their learning, pace their education, provide visually rich environments and create opportunities for interactions,' many Millennials recoil at the idea that they might be forced to endure classes geared to passive, auditory learners (Pletka, 2007: 54). Therefore, asking today's tech-savvy undergraduates to attend a boring, out-of-context library field-trip or to complete an old-fashioned, impossibly designed library scavenger hunt are incredibly ineffective methods for getting them interested in using a research library for almost any purpose. Indeed, what is especially concerning about many of the students new to our campuses today is their failure to recognize that there might be *any* need for or value to even entering the library building, much less enhancing their undeveloped library proficiencies (Burton and Chadwick, 2000; OCLC Online Computer Library Center, 2002; Gross and Latham, 2009). Unless these students' instructors understand their dependence upon technology, it is unlikely that today's Millennials will be convinced that information literacy has any relevance to their lives.

According to one study done by the Educational Testing Service (ETS) a mere 'thirteen percent of 3,000 college students and 800 high-school students' were able to demonstrate being reasonably 'information literate' (Foster, 2006: A36). Even though studies such as this show otherwise, students new to colleges and universities consistently tell librarians that they already know how to do research and that they are quite confident with their information-seeking techniques. The vast majority of Millennial students believe that information literacy competencies 'are skills everyone has, that growing up with computers provides these skills, and that what you need to know can be self-taught' (Gross and Latham, 2009: 346). Nevertheless, when Millennial students are tested, few can actually demonstrate the kind of information literacy proficiencies that their academic, professional or personal communities will eventually require of them.

High-school graduates who go off to attend institutions of higher education face a particularly steep learning curve because they have always seen 'the open space of the World Wide Web as their information universe,' and they have no idea that this view is likely to be in direct 'opposition to the worldview of librarians and many faculty, who perceive the library as the locus of information relevant to academic work' (Lippincott, 2005: 13.3). Any high-school graduate who has been trained to do research on the Internet by producing reports or by simply summarizing the information he or she finds on a topic is likely to have no idea that because these types of assignments are entirely non-evaluative, they set students up for failure in their first college-level courses. As Lippincott goes on to explain, while today's first-year students can usually 'multitask, learn systems without consulting manuals, and surf the Web, they lack technology and information skills appropriate for academic work.' Regrettably, the 'technology and information skills' emphasized by Lippincott are also the same proficiencies that she believes have never been integrated into most mainstream academic curricula (13.6). Therefore, many of our newest, most dependent, learners are often left to their own Internet-centered devices when it comes to locating the information sources they must rely upon to complete their academic assignments.

Students who lack the most basic of information literacy competencies quickly (and often painfully) make themselves obvious in their college classrooms. These are the four out of ten students who admit that 'they trust most or all online content' and demonstrate this trust by including only Internet sources of highly variable quality in their project bibliographies (Livingstone, 2008: 109). They are the two out of three teens who report having never 'been advised [about] how to judge the reliability of online information' and therefore rely only upon Procter & Gamble's company website for the information on which their research paper about the fat substitute Olestra is based (109). They are the self-assured students who refuse to ask academic librarians or their professors for research help because they believe that 'young people are better information seekers than older adults,' based on the notion 'that they [the young] grew up with the Internet' and as a result 'are more comfortable with computers and electronic sources than the older generation' (Gross and Latham, 2009: 345).

As Spence (2004) makes clear, these inexperienced undergraduates appear to their newly-met teaching faculty and academic librarians as having little, if any, meaningful critical judgment. As he puts it, they 'can locate landfills of information' and yet they have no idea how to gauge the relevance or reliability of this material. Even more importantly,

> It is not just a matter of judging sources; it is a matter of understanding what evidence, what examples, or what principles are needed to create a powerful argument. The process overwhelms thought. Their Googling produces more rambling pages sprinkled with graphics and drained of thought. (Spence, 2004: 488)

The unfortunate result of using a research process such as the one described above is a type of paper often referred to by the frustrated faculty members who read them as the data-dump. First-year students are particularly prone to this type of writing because they have not had enough practice gathering, analyzing or incorporating high-quality sources of information into their work. Additionally, because these novice researchers have had few if any opportunities in their pre-college years to learn about and use library tools, such resources appear too complex, too slow or too difficult to bother with. First-year students are entirely unprepared to practice the kind of research tenacity or deep reading regularly demonstrated by more experienced researchers. As Robert Kenedy and Vivienne Monty put it,

> Librarians can and must show students how to analyze information because it cannot be assumed that students are able to go from teacher-defined

purpose to understanding. Skills for critical and analytical use of information are seldom coached by faculties or the library, and this often results in recycled information rather than cognitively processed knowledge. (2008: 90)

As yet another college professor cleverly laments, 'geographically speaking, they [first-year students] are at home in the virtual world, uncomfortable in the alien wilds of the academic library, and downright terrified in the dark continent of the reference room' (Bankert and Van Vuuren, 2008: para. 1). Once these new students are asked to complete high-quality, college-level research, they come face to face with their utter lack of research experience. As a result of this harsh reality, many undergraduates develop some level of library anxiety. How better to avoid this painful learning experience than to quickly Google their way around the Internet?

Nevertheless, as Leticia Oseguera observes, even though Millennial students may not 'understand nor accept the need for [information literacy] instruction,' they absolutely need 'continued professional guidance' in order to understand that the mere 'availability of technology and [its] extended use . . . is not sufficient to instill information literacy' (2007: 45). By now, most academic librarians and teaching faculty realize that simply providing *access* to computers, networks and online information services does not instantaneously create successful researchers, accomplished critical thinkers or particularly good paper writers. We also know, as Leamnson observes, that 'when it comes to freshmen, neither learning nor teaching can be made effortless' (2003: 82). The central question then becomes, how can teaching faculty and academic librarians work together to provide our newest, least experienced students with the information literacy education they require in order to become truly successful lifelong learners?

Another of the challenges facing those of us who are non-digital natives and who currently work with novice researchers has been an inclination to confuse information literacy competencies with these new students' seemingly superior prowess at manipulating existing popular technologies. While it is certainly important to recognize that most new undergraduates have a great proclivity for operating in today's technological milieu, in isolation such expertise has little to do with the deeper, lifelong, problem-solving abilities most academicians hope to instill in their students. Educating college students to be information literate requires that neither teaching faculty nor academic librarians regard a 'child who "whizzes" around the screen' as 'so skilled that, we conclude comfortably, they know all they need to know already' (Livingstone, 2008: 101). As Ito et al. (2010) report (and many adults instinctually recognize), most adolescents today are not using their new technological tools to access consequential information resources as a way of enriching their academic careers. Rather, 'the majority of youth use new media to "hang out" and extend existing friendships' (Ito et al., 2010: 1). In their report, funded by the John D. and Catherine T. MacArthur Foundation, Ito et al. conclude that:

> Contemporary social media are becoming one of the primary 'institutions' of peer culture for U.S. teens, occupying the role that was previously dominated by the informal hanging out spaces of the school, mall, home, or street. Further, much of this engagement is centered on access to social and commercial entertainment content that is generally *frowned upon in formal educational settings*. (2010: 35, emphasis added)

Susan Herring's work further corroborates this typical adolescent tech behavior. She writes, 'Young people use new technologies for social ends that are much the same as for earlier generations using old technologies' (2008: 77). Therefore no matter how tech-savvy these young students may be in terms of managing their personal lives, many of the K-12 educational settings they have experienced in the United States, 'remain relatively unchanged by the information era,' a condition which for some students helps foster early academic disengagement (Pletka, 2007: 16, 19). While certainly not all incoming first-year students enter higher education disengaged from learning, it is clear that most of these same young people have managed to incorporate popular technologies much more seamlessly into their personal lives than we as educators have managed to in our curricula.

What to do with these multidimensional first-year students in what to them appears to be a dusty, boring, old library? Studies show that while these novice researchers may be academically 'ill-prepared' to live up to the many assumptions made by their college professors, they are also 'inquisitive, savvy, demanding, and increasingly independent information seekers' (Leamnson, 2003: 36; Connaway et al., 2008: 132). At the same time that they are practicing 'academic promiscuity, a kind of textual sleeping around among whatever attractive sources' can be quickly and effortlessly located, they are also 'developing new forms of media literacy that are keyed to new media and youth-centered social and cultural worlds' (Burton and Chadwick, 2000: 309–10; Ito et al., 2010: 37). Because so many first-year students are simply unable to find the necessary resources, 'they cannot solve problems,' and yet, these same students come to us expecting classrooms 'where digital affordances and tools enable engagement in self-directed activities, and [where] learners exercise agency in moving beyond mere participation in communities of inquiry to become active creators of ideas, resources, and knowledge artifacts' (Spence, 2004: 491; McLoughlin and Lee, 2008: 14). Which is to say, today's first-year students remain enigmatic. They come unprepared for the rigors of academia and they regularly reject conventional educational pedagogies. They have absolutely no concept of the deep, critical thinking that will be required of them not only while they matriculate, but upon graduation as well. According to Orme, today's 'first-year students are similar to immigrants to a new country,' which suggests that 'it is incumbent upon members of the higher education community to explain the new culture and the unique and central role that information plays in academic culture' (2008: 69). This assimilatory work is greatly enhanced when teaching faculty and academic librarians work together to directly engage students in meaningful research work in the library.

As an important and lasting set of abilities, information literacy and the critical thinking it necessitates take time to develop and require expert guidance and a great deal of hands-on practice. The instruction presenting information literacy concepts cannot be relegated to one-shot, out-of-context library sessions. As Spence reports, simply 'creating library assignments as add-ons to courses' quickly results in 'student hostility' toward the library and its resources (2004: 491). Students today are too often disengaged by this outmoded pedagogical approach. Consequently, rather than downplay it, teaching faculty and academic librarians would do well to harness this group of students' interest in technology. Livingstone enthusiastically supports this teaching strategy, remarking that 'celebrating young people's enterprise and enthusiasm, while failing to support, respond, or engage with their online activities, risks failing to bring to fruition the ambitious hopes we hold not only for the internet but, more significantly, for young people' (2008: 117). Providing first-year students with carefully integrated, meaningful, library-based opportunities that ask them to practice evaluating the information they plan to use in the completion of their coursework may seem yet another labor-intensive burden being laid at the teaching faculty's instructional door. Yet, according to many academic librarians (and the author of this book), that belief really is unfounded.

Process-centered library research

Some years ago, a young student approached the reference desk where I was working and asked if I could help her find some statistics about China. This young woman further explained that she was currently taking our institution's equivalent of the first-year composition course and that she had been asked by her professor to write a ten to twelve-page argumentative, researched paper. The reason she had finally come to me, she said, was that she had been searching on the Internet for a long time and was having trouble finding statistical resources for China. After a little more discussion with this student, she shared the news flash with me that she really had very little interest in her paper topic. However, she had found picking a paper topic for this course *very* difficult and her instructor had already spent quite a lot of time with her negotiating a workable thesis statement. Now, she told me, what she absolutely needed were some statistical resources that would show there was soon to be a major population explosion in China. Always the dutiful reference librarian, I began to help her dig around a bit to see what we could find. Because the Internet was a relatively new resource at the time, I began our hunt by first looking through our library's print reference collection. We soon found that our library's collection had several great resources in which population statistics (current and projected) were reported by country, China included. But, just as I began to congratulate myself on my research acumen, the student got a horror-struck look on her face. What was the cause for her concern? Rather than showing an impending population explosion, each of the print statistical sources we located clearly projected a *decline* in China's population over time. The student was devastated. She said that she had told her professor that her paper was going to be on the population explosion that was going to happen in China and that he told her it was a good idea for a paper so THAT is what she was going to have to write for him. I tried to console this young woman by telling her that what was more likely to happen was that her professor would be pleased to know that she had learned something new about her area of research. I tried to impress upon her that the purpose of all research projects was to find exciting, new information that would help answer her research questions and impact her thinking about an issue. But, this student was having none of that. She angrily asked me if we couldn't 'just go on to the Internet and find some statistics that DO show there would be a Chinese population explosion?!' I was dumbfounded and again tried to gently explain to her that if the several reputable sources we had located in print (with publishers such as the United Nations Statistical Division, the Central Intelligence Agency, and *Statesman's Yearbook*, etc.) all said the same thing, it was very unlikely that she could prove something that was not borne out by this data. As I began to reiterate the idea that the main purpose of writing a research paper was to learn and say something new, the full truth finally emerged. The student was furious and told me that she did not have time to spend 'on this stuff' because her paper was due in two days and she had to find ten sources and get it written. As she stomped off, she huffed that she would go back to the Internet and 'just find some stuff there.'

This student taught me (in a particularly distressing way) a number of things about first-year students and their preconceived notions about research. Of course, this interaction was disturbing on many levels. But, what was most blatantly apparent was that this student had no sense of her library work as being a part of what more experienced researchers know is often a lengthy, entirely recursive process. This student saw her research paper experience as yet another educational hoop through which to jump. She simply wanted to complete this bothersome leap as quickly and effortlessly as possible. In fact she, not unlike hundreds of the new students I have worked with over the years, began this paper using the typical linear thinking that is so prevalent amongst first-year students. She saw the paper project as moving straight from a thesis statement (which she admitted her professor essentially provided) to quickly collecting a few library items (which she had no experience doing and no interest in reading) to somehow writing an A-grade paper. In this student's mind the question likely became, 'How long can this boring routine possibly take?' rather than, 'What can I learn and say about this topic that is interesting and new?'

With the growing dependence on the Internet's speed and ease, as well as the continued lack of information literacy competency among high-school graduates, most academic librarians can tell you that this linear, extremely utilitarian thinking has become particularly problematic for many new students. Even at institutions where teaching faculty and academic librarians actively work together, first-year students continue to struggle to extract themselves from the 'need to respond in a way that will maximize [their] grade, or at least allow [them] to pass, rather than focusing on what is being learned' (Gross and Latham, 2009: 342). This persistent need to 'focus on assignment requirements rather than on asking meaningful questions' becomes extremely challenging when teaching faculty and librarians ask these novice researchers 'to *use* information – to apply, synthesize, question, understand, and communicate' (Bowles-Terry et al., 2010: 229–30). Gross and Latham's study maintains that, for most young students, 'successful information seeking need only be measured by the ability to *find* the information, not the *process used to get there*' (Gross and Latham, 2009: 341, emphasis added). It is therefore increasingly important that we as instructors clearly articulate rigorous expectations for external source usage and library research. We must also be sure to actively demonstrate this work as a progressive process of discovery, one that takes time and will likely cause some discomfort and frustration at certain stages.

How exactly then, does an undergraduate's research process work? Do these students even *have* a research process? According to one preliminary investigation described by Barbara Fister, one-size-fits-all answers to these questions are hard to come by. Fister's 1992 article, 'The Research Processes of Undergraduate Students,' is an early call for academic librarians and teaching faculty to more closely examine their students' library research activities. As a result of interviews she did with a number of older, more successful undergraduate researchers, Fister found that rather than provide 'library instruction that deals with finding materials' and emphasizes 'a sequential, tool-oriented search technique,' students needed to understand that 'research is not a straightforward application of tools in a systematic fashion, but an interplay of a variety of factors in which information collection plays an integrated part' (1992: 163, 164). Fister explains,

> Leaving students to flounder on their own – or simply teaching the skills required to find materials for a single library-related assignment – is not doing justice to our students or to the educational aims of our institutions. Furthermore, it doesn't make sense to teach disparate library skills without putting them in the context of the research process. The students in our classrooms want to see some pattern behind the skills, want to see how the pieces fit together. (Fister, 1992: 164)

As an early advocate for extending the examination of the undergraduate research process, Fister is likely heartened by the significant work that has been done in this area since her initial study. Today, a great deal of theoretical writing which examines how students process their learning in an academic library setting exists within the field of library and information science (LIS). Should teaching faculty wish to explore this rich literature further, William Orme's book chapter, titled 'Information Literacy and First-Year Students,' provides a nice overview of some of the more up-to-date, resultant literature. In particular, Orme's piece examines two research foci which have intersected to generate quite a lot of recent investigative interest within academic libraries: first, there is the emphasis higher education now places on increasing first-year student success; and second, the development of a more holistic approach for bringing about information literacy across the student body (Orme, 2008). Orme identifies a number of seminal works upon which contemporary thinking about information literacy education continues to be based and concludes his chapter by writing,

It is important for students to gain new knowledge, but it is perhaps more important for the higher education community to pay greater attention to the nature of knowledge and how it is gained. If those issues are explicitly addressed as part of a first-year curriculum along with the necessary mechanics and resources attendant in a university setting, the foundations can be set in place to support the type of lifelong learning that information literacy advocates have promised. (Orme, 2008: 70)

Orme reiterates the increasing importance information literacy has as a universal teaching and learning issue at institutions of higher education. It is his belief that the growing body of research addressing the academic value of information literacy competency, especially in the case of first-year students, continues to legitimize the need for all educational institutions to further develop, strengthen and extend the curricular reach of their library instruction programs.

Unfortunately, however, one important information literacy advocate that Orme chooses not to include in his review is Carol Collier Kuhlthau. Kuhlthau is perhaps the librarian scholar best known for her work identifying and closely examining student research practices. Her highly influential 'Information Search Process' (ISP) model focuses on what she demonstrated to be the six stages of research (see Figure 2.1). Each of these stages includes cognitive, physical and affective dimensions (Kuhlthau et al., 2008: para. 3). Kuhlthau identifies these progressive phases as: 'initiation,' 'selection,' 'exploration,' 'formulation,' 'collection,' and 'presentation' (2004: 82).

A brief textual explanation of each phase can be found in Figure 2.2.

| Figure 2.1 | Kuhlthau's Information Search Process (ISP) model |

Model of the Information Search Process

	Initiation	Selection	Exploration	Formulation	Collection	Presentation	Assessment
Feelings (Affective)	Uncertainty	Optimism	Confusion Frustration Doubt	Clarity	Sense of direction / Confidence	Satisfaction or Disappointment	Sense of accomplishment
Thoughts (Cognitive)	vague ———————→			focused	increased	interest	Increased self-awareness
Actions (Physical)	seeking	relevant Exploring	information	seeking	pertinent Documenting	information	

| Figure 2.2 | Kuhlthau's six ISP stages |

- *Initiation*, when a person first becomes aware of a lack of knowledge or understanding and feelings of uncertainty and apprehension are common.

- *Selection*, when a general area, topic, or problem is identified and initial uncertainty often gives way to a brief sense of optimism and a readiness to begin the search.

- *Exploration*, when inconsistent, incompatible information is encountered and uncertainty, confusion, and doubt frequently increase and people find themselves 'in the dip' of confidence.

- *Formulation*, when a focused perspective is formed and uncertainty diminishes as confidence begins to increase.

- *Collection*, when information pertinent to the focused perspective is gathered and uncertainty subsides as interest and involvement deepens.

- *Presentation*, when the search is completed with a new understanding enabling the person to explain his or her learning to others or in someway (sic) put the learning to use.

Source: http://comminfo.rutgers.edu/~kuhlthau/information_search_process.htm

Unsurprisingly, Kuhlthau's research shows that the more complex the information-seeking task, the more uncertainty students feel. If, however, teaching faculty and academic librarians can intervene in a timely manner and purposely guide students through these earlier phases to a point of 'focus formulation,' the interest that students show in their projects often increases and frustration levels eventually decline (Kuhlthau et al., 2008: para. 6). Furthermore, Kuhlthau's work explains that the increase of insecurity most students feel during the earliest phases of their research is 'frequently unexpected,' and she notes that this frustration often causes 'apprehension and confusion in some searchers to the point of obstructing the task' (Kuhlthau et al., 2008: para. 3). As academic librarians can attest, this library frustration and anxiety, particularly among first-year students, is damaging and real (Van Scoyoc, 2003; Onwuegbuzie et al., 2004; Malvasi et al., 2009). Fister's work corroborates this caution, having noted a great deal of trepidation amongst even the upper-class students in her study as they tried to negotiate a focus for their research. As she puts it, rather than seeing this phase of research as merely a 'frightening and unproductive' ordeal, academic librarians and teaching faculty 'need to forewarn them [students] that developing a focus takes time and is a creative and somewhat intuitive process' (Fister, 1992: 168). In her book *Seeking Meaning*, Kuhlthau reiterates the importance of treating this affective phenomenon seriously.

> Uncertainty, the predominant experience in the early stages of the information search process, is not being sufficiently addressed in library and information services. The uncertainty principle states that uncertainty is a cognitive state that commonly causes affective symptoms of anxiety and lack of confidence. Uncertainty and anxiety can be expected in the early stages of the [research] process. (Kuhlthau, 2004: 200)

Such affective, and, in some cases, physical dimensions of the undergraduate research process can confound even the brightest of students. This is why Kuhlthau advocates her ISP model for teaching faculty and librarians as a guide to recognizing the most 'critical moments when instructional interventions are essential in students' information-to-knowledge experiences' (Kuhlthau et al., 2008: para. 9). In Kuhlthau's opinion, the timing of any information literacy session is, therefore, equally as important as its content.

As her work is refined over time, studies continue to show that Kuhlthau's model 'remains a useful research tool for designing, framing and analyzing the investigation of information seeking behaviour in complex tasks and also continues to be useful for designing user centred [*sic*] information services and systems particularly for students in inquiry projects' (Kuhlthau et al., 2008: para. 36). Yet, though it might prove immensely helpful to most new students as a framework for their earliest academic research projects, very few first-year undergraduates (or teaching faculty for that matter) are likely to hear about, much less delve into Kuhlthau's ISP model to any extent. This is likely to be true even if students do receive a few library sessions as part of their first-year writing courses. Why is this so? The truth is that today, most academic librarians remain constrained from taking a more global or theoretical, process-based approach to information literacy by institutional, curricular or even pedagogical obstacles. If this seems a somewhat petulant comment from a grumpy academic librarian, consider the following illustrative and all-too-common real-life examples: a well-meaning faculty member vaguely asks a librarian colleague to teach his students 'how to use the library' in a single 50-minute class period; a sheepish instructor schedules a library session for her class on the one day she is planning to be out of town, attending an academic conference; a new adjunct creates an overly ambitious library-based assignment for his large first-year course without ever having tested it in the library from the perspective of an unsophisticated, novice researcher or having arranged an opportunity for these new students to receive library instruction. Such situations continue to pose challenges for many academic librarians, who often have little choice but to take whatever course-time teaching faculty feel they can spare. Though most librarians know it is simply impossible for first-year undergraduates to leave a single 'one-shot' library session sporting a sound process-based framework upon which to base their future library work, most do try to understand the increasing pressures facing teaching faculty as well. While most academic librarians work hard to get over being grumpy about these less-than-ideal library instruction opportunities, many of us also continue to have significant concerns about the impacts such brief and out-of-context interactions really have on students.

To one extent or another, circumstances such as the ones described above are in existence at most academic institutions. Academic librarians know that today's extraordinarily busy faculty members are likely to have good reasons for having inadvertently helped create them. We also know that these kinds of non-collaborative situations cut both ways. They are often the result of a well-intentioned but unsystematic library instruction program whereby 'Individual tutoring by instructors and librarians gets some students functioning, but many get lost, never to explore the possibilities of systematic research' (Spence, 2004: 491). Susan Carol Curzon categorizes these types of library instruction programs as having been based on the 'On-Demand Model,' and notes that though it is the 'prevailing model in most libraries today,' there are some significant problems with the format (2004: 43). According to Curzon, the two key disadvantages of this program type are that 'information literacy instruction is often only an hour or two,' and the model utilizes a 'hit-or-miss strategy, with the result that some students go through their entire educational career without the important ingredient of information literacy training' (43). While there has recently been an increase in the literature describing effective information literacy collaborations between individual librarians and teaching faculty, the historic model of offering 'one or two library instruction sessions' per introductory composition or first-year experience course continues to dominate most academic library program models (Misangyi Watts, 2005: 341). According to Misangyi Watts,

> This model has been the mainstay of instruction efforts, yet its effectiveness is ambiguous. As the needs to address critical skills, such as search strategy, database structure, and database manipulation, have increased, the success of the model has been questioned. One or two 'how to library' sessions do not provide sufficient time to address the affective, cognitive, and behavior domains for learning. (2005: 342)

She continues that if academic librarians hope to 'figure into the overall educational goals of any college or university,' then library instruction programming, especially that which is intentionally geared toward first-year students, 'must be understood in the context of the total activities of the student, the library, and the curriculum' (344). Academic librarians who want to build strong library instruction programs must closely collaborate with teaching faculty in order to devise creative ways in which students who are new to the academy can engage in constructivist information literacy learning early in their academic careers. It is important to teach our newest students how to 'engage in active cognitive processing, such as paying attention to relevant incoming information, mentally organizing incoming information into a coherent representation, and mentally integrating incoming information with existing knowledge' (Anderson et al., 2001: 65). If we expect our highly connected, tech-crazy undergraduates to reengage with what they see as 'imposed information seeking in the form of school assignments', we must give them assignments that are meaningful and relevant to their lives (Gross and Latham, 2009: 342). In addition, the 'core intent' of any information literacy program 'needs to be engaging students to become information literate in both formal and informal ways' (Misangyi Watts, 2005: 344). Bruce agrees, noting that

> Learning opportunities that enhance information literacy not only make use of information and communication infrastructures, but are designed to bring the information practices, that are effective in professional, civic and personal life into [*sic*] curriculum. . . . When reflection on learning to be information literate is added to the experience of information literacy, students are helped to recognize the transferability of the processes involved to everyday life, community and workplace contexts. (Bruce, 2004: para. 4)

Creating these types of meaningful, holistic, integrative information literacy programs has proven difficult. First-year students at most institutions of higher education today continue to have wildly differing experiences with academic librarians and library research. This means, for example, that when I visit with teaching faculty about information literacy at my own institution, my first advice is never to expect any kind of consistently significant research experience from students, especially when students are enrolled as first-year or sophomore undergraduates. Even when these students say they already know how to do research (and they will most certainly claim that they do), it does not mean that they will be equipped to meet their professor's academic research expectations.

As I have already described, for most first-year students, developing the many aptitudes necessary to efficiently and effectively complete even the most basic of researched academic papers takes a great deal of time, guidance and practice. Moreover, the reality that academic papers require work that is often unfamiliar, protracted and far from effortless is not likely to be popular news to new undergraduates:

> Researching a hypothesis requires skill and discipline. An organized argument that sustains a knowledge claim requires precise information, careful definitions, and nuanced judgment of reliability. All that means students must learn an effective library search process and spend hours of practice. The costs are time, drudgery, and failures. The rewards of successful craft and care come at the end of a long process. (Spence, 2004: 487)

Despite Spence's rather dark and gloomy description above, there is a positive side here too. For, as difficult as the vision of achieving true information literacy competency among college and university undergraduates may initially seem to all involved, each of us comes to this work uniquely well suited to take it on. Today's teaching faculty are distinctively prepared and well situated to further the aims of any information literacy competency agenda. Talented educators come to their institutions after having gained important

70

expertise in their disciplines and specialties. College and university professors have developed through a 'long process of acculturation,' an 'in-depth knowledge of the discipline, awareness of important scholars working in particular areas, participation in a system of informal scholarly communication, and a view of research as a non-sequential, non-linear process with a large degree of ambiguity and serendipity' (Leckie, 1996: 202). Academic librarians, too, have confidence in the value of our contribution to the information literacy endeavor. We appreciate that our purpose and roles have dramatically changed over time. With the rapid advance of electronic information tools, we understand that we are no longer meant to be staid guardians of the academy's research. Accordingly, academic librarians can help teaching faculty soften Spence's dire message for their newest, most vulnerable learners. In fact, we are eager to be involved with this process because, as Leckie notes, 'at some point in the student's educational experience, there must be a convergence of both information and disciplinary literacy if true learning is to be facilitated' (1996: 206). We are, therefore, serious about working with teaching faculty to engage students in meaningful ways with the many indispensable research strategies and important information tools that these newcomers will need as college students, recent graduates and lifelong learners.

Teaching faculty and academic librarians need to capitalize more effectively on our shared educational mission. Because we are natural allies in so many ways, we need to talk about our academic fields more and see if we cannot further identify intersections and practical ways in which we might further support one another's work. Though our individual specialties often lead us down divergent disciplinary, pedagogical and investigative paths, we all want our students to be engaged by, excited about and experienced in the processes involved with true inquiry, whatever path they decide to take.

> This process of inquiry includes seeking, refining, seeking again, modification of a question, and so forth. All are a part of using databases, navigating websites, and checking out a myriad of sources for finding information. Just as higher education has become less about rote and more about a learning process, so too has the library, in the sense that one appreciates the process of asking and seeking and evaluating information. (Misangyi Watts, 2005: 352)

When teaching faculty and academic librarians collaborate to ensure novice researchers are adequately supported during each phase of authentic, inquiry-based research projects, good things are more likely to happen than when these students are left to struggle trying to gather information sources on their own. Of course not all collaborations result in immediate, unmitigated success. Such collaborative work isn't always comfortable, and it takes time and effort to develop instructional strategies which work to further both information literacy competencies and disciplinary outcomes. Yet, if our newest students see no evidence that the courses they take and the research assignments they must complete are guiding them 'toward the authentic and normative conceptions that reflect the most commonly accepted and *best current knowledge and thinking* in the academic disciplines and subject matter areas' (Anderson and Krathwohl, 2001: 38, emphasis added), then the mission of higher education will fail for us all. More simply stated (with apologies to George Carlin), in today's rapidly changing, information-saturated world, we all must be able to efficiently and effectively find stuff. Our most vulnerable undergraduate learners desperately need to learn how to find *good* stuff. If we as teaching faculty and academic librarians do not work together to teach these students the necessary processes of locating, evaluating and using high-quality stuff, who will?

How can course content and information literacy co-exist?

In an article that at points seems a bit fractious, William B. Badke (2005) takes on an especially thorny issue, one that continues to be difficult for academic librarians and teaching faculty to navigate. At the center of this disagreement is a fundamental 'perception of the lack of time,' which Hardesty describes as 'a particular characteristic of faculty culture' and which over time seems to have been greatly amplified (1995: para. 65). Because teaching faculty have long enjoyed 'complete professional autonomy' in respect to their classrooms, academic librarians have been required to find ways for faculty to participate in library instruction programming in 'as time efficient [a manner] as possible;' a restriction that is not always an easy nor the most effective criterion to satisfy (Hardesty, 1995: para. 61; Jenkins, 2005: 60). Badke's discussion of this issue begins with an observation that academic librarians tend to focus more heavily on process, while teaching faculty often place more emphasis on course content (2005: 63). He goes on to suggest that these incongruous educational positions tend to work mainly against academic librarians because librarians 'are locked within an environment in which discipline-specific instruction is the norm, professors cling to their turf, and the powers that be will release neither personnel, funding nor curriculum space to enable a wider information literacy enterprise to take root' (71). Badke writes that while most members of teaching faculties continue to 'rate library research instruction as very important,' the enduring perception that integrating information literacy outcomes into their course will require a significant loss of disciplinary content remains a serious limitation (64). The result of this difference of opinion has been that many teaching faculty continue to view library instruction as entirely skills-based, optional, and therefore 'a small blip on the radar' (70). As another librarian more helpfully puts it, 'faculty generally agree on the importance of information literacy, but need more of a push to truly embrace it within the curriculum' (DaCosta, 2010: 203–4). Unfortunately, because most academic librarians' curricular influence is minimal, we usually have very little muscle with which to push. This lack of curricular authority leads to the view among many librarians that the campus library continues to be 'a tremendous educational resource that is not fulfilling its potential' (Hardesty, 1995: para. 108). Increasingly, academic librarians worry that our patrons struggle mightily with information overload and a growing form of 'intellectual poverty' precisely because these students (and some teaching faculty) suffer from modern-day research inexperience and are therefore unable to efficiently or effectively utilize contemporary library research tools (para. 108).

In an article published in 2006, Claire McGuinness describes a study she did on 'faculty attitudes specifically towards information literacy development' (2006: 575). While her investigation took place in the Republic of Ireland, the results of McGuinness' work further reinforced earlier assertions about faculty culture made by prominent American researchers as well (Hardesty, 1995; Badke, 2005). The purpose of McGuinness' qualitative study was to examine the 'perceptions, beliefs and practices' of Irish teaching faculty and to identify 'areas of conflict and culture clash that may hinder the establishment of [information literacy] programs' (McGuinness, 2006: 576). Unfortunately, the attitudinal impediments identified by McGuinness during her interviews with Irish teaching faculty continue their entrenchment in certain segments of the American academy today. According to McGuinness' work, most teaching faculty report subscribing to one or more of the following theories:

1. *The Heads in the Sand Theory*: There continue to be teaching faculty who believe that they are *already* teaching information literacy competencies well enough, thank you very much. McGuinness reports that among the faculty she surveyed, 'there was a tacit assumption . . . that students would somehow absorb and develop the requisite knowledge and skills through the very process of preparing a piece of written coursework' (577). While these teaching faculty do not explicitly articulate information literacy outcomes for their courses or show their students how to find academic research with any intentionality, they nevertheless believe that they are currently doing a good enough job at getting students into the library.

2. *The Sink or Swim Theory*: McGuinness found that some teaching faculty believe that whether or not a student becomes information literate 'depends almost entirely on personal interest, individual motivation and innate ability, rather than on the quality and format of the available instructional opportunities' (577). These faculty members may rely on antiquated memories of their own formative library experiences relying on the assumption that since they were able to figure library research out on their own, today's Millennial students will certainly be able to do the same.

3. *The Osmosis Theory*: Finally, McGuinness identified teaching faculty who seem to feel that having a formal

structure for promoting information literacy is unnecessary. Rather, these faculty members see information literacy competency as a 'natural, almost intuitive process, whereby students will somehow work it out for themselves through encountering and resolving information problems throughout the course of their education' (578). These faculty members are confident that their students attain information literacy proficiency and yet, these professors are usually, 'unable to explain the mechanism by which it occurs' (578).

McGuinness includes two additional pedagogically related findings in her article. First, she documents teaching faculty who believe that most students 'learn how to be information literate mainly through working with their fellow students and turning to their peers,' and second, she identifies faculty who believe that information literacy competency seems to naturally evolve as a result 'of being confronted with an unfamiliar situation or a seemingly intractable information problem' (579). For these last faculty members, the often haphazard technique of painstakingly 'working out how to achieve a satisfactory solution or find an appropriate answer to a question' is the main method responsible for imparting information literacy competencies among their students (579).

Certainly there have been excellent improvements made to information literacy programming at numerous institutions of higher education since McGuinness' article was originally published. Yet, for many academic librarians these discouraging attitudinal findings remain the 600-pound gorilla in certain academic departments. Regrettably, DaCosta makes the transatlantic 'information literacy skills gap' even more obvious after comparing faculty perceptions toward information literacy in the United States and England as recently as May 2010 (2010: 217). DaCosta's literature review concludes with the remark that, while information literacy education may be very important to academic librarians all over the world, it 'does not illustrate a wider acceptance and adoption within higher education in general' (204).

Clearly, presumptions such as those expressed by *The Heads in the Sand Theory, The Sink or Swim Theory* or *The Osmosis Theory* have proven difficult to dislodge from the minds of some teaching faculty. Unhelpful as they are, unfounded theories such as these have long been in existence, and they continue to hamper faculty–librarian collaboration and information literacy programming at institutions of all sizes. Academic librarians who dispute such conventional assumptions know that if Millennial students are ever going to truly understand 'the nature of knowledge and how it is gained,' faculty and librarians must be more intentional about communicating (with one another and their first-year students) exactly what high-quality academic research looks like in today's information-rich world (Orme, 2008: 70).

Regrettably, uncertain portrayals (such as those noted above) of the potential for authentic collaboration between academic librarians and teaching faculty members are all too common. Yet, it should be clear that this author does *not* believe that disagreements over disciplinary content and the inclusion of information literacy outcomes need be an insurmountable dilemma. Nor do I believe the promise of close collaboration is a Pollyannaish view. As Jenkins notes, academic librarians today have great respect for their teaching colleagues, but we cannot afford to fear them or students will suffer (2005: 35). Collaborations, therefore, can arise because academic librarians understand their faculty's distinct culture and empathize with them based in part on this mutual sense of responsibility to students.

Academic librarians today do understand that our teaching faculty may be 'used to working independently' and we also recognize the demanding nature of an academic's work life (Jenkins, 2005: 35). We remember, for the most part, that our professors do 'recognize and respect the library's mission' but that they 'may not always have time to strictly follow its [the library's] procedures' (Jenkins, 2005: 35). In my own experience, all of this knowledge has meant that I approach busy faculty members with proposals that are as student-focused and as mutually beneficial as I can possibly make them. Using this strategy has meant that I have yet to meet the faculty member who absolutely refuses any and all respectful suggestions for ways to ensure that students struggle less with their research work, are able to accomplish more in an academic library and ultimately improve their performance on research-based assignments. As Hardesty notes,

> Many faculty do create imaginative and educationally productive assignments involving student use of the library, consult with librarians in the development of those assignments, and invite librarians into their classrooms to provide instruction and guidance to students in the use of the academic library. (Hardesty, 1995: para. 107)

Academic librarians have a wealth of simple information literacy content ideas and effective, time-saving pedagogical techniques that, once judiciously shared with teaching faculty, are often greatly appreciated. Ultimately, even those early collaboration attempts that need more time to evolve can be positive experiences if academic librarians and teaching faculty communicate with care and respect one another's many professional gifts and challenges.

Christine Bruce has written that 'an effective information literacy education requires explicit attention to information processes; as well as the careful crafting of real world information practices, and meaningful reflection, into curricula' (2004: para. 21). Misangyi Watts subscribes to this notion as well, further observing that if institutions wish to instigate a successful information literacy program based on best practice pedagogies, such a program must be sure that it 'supports multiple approaches to teaching and learning, is strong on active learning, encompasses critical thinking and reflection, and links course work to the real-world experiences of students' (2005: 349). Demonstrating their process-centered approaches, these two librarian authors are advocating for information literacy work that is closely tied to the curriculum and to what they call 'real-world' information literacy concepts. Library research assignments which do neither of these two things are, for most academic librarians, extremely easy to spot. One such unfortunate example follows.

Many years ago, as a newly minted reference librarian, I was cautioned to watch for a particular assignment given by Professor X. At least two of my more experienced colleagues had worked with this assignment previously. They assured me that the assignment was a perennial event and that, unhappily, it was also a dreadful experience on many levels. From my own experience, I knew Professor X was an active scholar, a dedicated teacher and, best of all, a really nice person. His first-year students seemed to really enjoy the courses he taught. Though he had a rather unconventional (and somewhat disquieting) way of introducing students to an academic library (he liked to bring them into the building for a class period when he suggested that they wander around 'experiencing' the library), I genuinely liked this fellow and confidently thought to myself, 'Well, how bad could this assignment be, really?' I soon learned that the assignment Professor X chose to give new students as a means of further introducing them to the library was a scavenger hunt. In fact, it was no ordinary scavenger hunt. This assignment was a lengthy, infuriatingly vague, virtually impossible undertaking which had no apparent connection to either the content of the course or to teaching new undergraduates how to actually use their academic library. This assignment asked brand-new first-year students to answer approximately 20 esoteric, highly specific, factual questions. One question that caused particular consternation required students to identify the four major classes of fire and to provide a brief description of each. Today a quick search of the Internet makes answering this question a breeze. But back then it was nearly impossible for even the most experienced members of the library faculty to locate a source in our reference collection that provided an acceptable answer for the 24 students who came in one after another requesting it. Later, upon carefully questioning Professor X about his intended outcomes for the assignment, he told me that he thought it was a 'fun' way for students who were new to our campus to learn about the library. Though I was not nearly brave enough to tell him so at the time, there was absolutely *nothing* about this assignment that could even remotely be described as fun for either his students or his friendly reference librarians.

I have often wondered about the reasoning behind this type of assignment. Completing an exercise such as the one described above is much like going into a large, brand-new grocery store for the very first time, while on a tight schedule. How *fun* is it really to try to procure the needed items from a lengthy list when you have no idea how the store is organized and are already running late? At least in a grocery store it is reasonable to assume that most shoppers encounter a general arrangement scheme which they have seen at other grocery stores and with which they have some familiarity. But the vast majority of today's first-year students have no conception of how an academic library is physically arranged. Many Millennial students have never even set foot in their local public library. Even those who have used their school or public libraries are in trouble because they are used to locating items based on the Dewey Decimal Classification (DDC) system rather than the Library of Congress Classification (LCC) system, which is used by most academic libraries in the United States.

The deeper issue with this scavenger assignment, however, was that Professor X provided no context for its relevance or value, either within the course itself or for the information research process. This assignment misses the mark in many ways, but, as Misangyi Watts notes, it misses primarily because it has no authentic, course-integrated application:

> The goal is to give first-year students the tools with which to navigate scholarly narratives, understand discourse as a conversation over time, and take part in critically assessing and evaluating information. Students should still be invited to go to the library, ask a librarian, or browse a collection, but this should now be anchored in an overall collaborative approach to helping students understand both how and why they need to be information literate. (Misangyi Watts, 2005: 340)

First-year students taking Professor X's composition courses regularly came to the reference desk close to tears. Many wandered endlessly around the library's reference collection, unsuccessfully pulling random volumes off shelves, hoping to locate the answer to questions which were too specific or arcane for the *World Book Encyclopedia* or the *Encyclopaedia Britannica*.

What did these students learn that they could apply to their writing course? In truth, they may have gained some, minimal affective benefit from this ordeal. They learned how fast the reference librarians could find the answers to their professor's questions and how eager these professionals were to help them. As a result, they may have also decided which of the librarians they would go to if they ever again had a really hard factual question and were absolutely desperate for assistance. Yet, according to Professor X himself, the main goal of this scavenger hunt was to introduce students to the library in a fun and entertaining way. What did these students actually learn about the library? They learned that it was frustrating and excruciatingly hard to use. They learned that even when they did stumble across something useful, the process involved was exceptionally time-consuming and unsatisfying. They learned that if there was any way that they could *avoid* using this huge (to them), imposing and impossible-to-understand building during the remainder of their undergraduate career, they would work hard to undertake it. Eventually, those first-year students who tried to complete this assignment somewhat closer to its due-date also learned that members of the exasperated reference staff were not above subverting the entire search process by making photocopies of a completed scavenger hunt worksheet and simply handing out copies. Rather than carefully incorporating authentic information literacy outcomes into his composition class, Professor X managed to contrive a completely artificial assignment which had no relevance to his students' course-work and no positive, measurable impacts on his students' library research capabilities. Therefore, these students quickly labeled the scavenger hunt as unimportant, busy-work. This kind, smart, dedicated teacher did 'a good job – albeit unintentionally – of making sure [his] students remain[ed] information illiterate' (Breivik,

82

2005: 24). Worst of all, this assignment was given quite early in these first-year students' academic career, essentially ensuring that their first interaction with the library was a frustratingly negative one and as a result they would not soon return. A valuable opening for meaningful information literacy work was therefore tightly closed from the start.

How might this faculty member have improved his students' library learning experience? He could have consulted an academic librarian prior to issuing his scavenger hunt assignment. To those of us in the profession, suggesting that teaching faculty might want to regularly check in with their academic librarians seems exceedingly obvious. Librarians remain mystified when research assignments that have apparently been designed ad hoc, with no consideration for the library's actual collections or the institution's most inexperienced researchers, appear before us. How could this professor have asked his/her students to use resource X when the library has not owned it for almost five years? How could this faculty member have possibly thought that requiring all 35 of her/his students to use the same print periodical index, without showing them where it is located or how to use it, was a good idea? Why did this professor include instructions for using the CD-ROM version of this database in his/her syllabus when we have had the Internet-based version for more than a year? How could this faculty member have expected first-year students to use an advanced disciplinary periodical index to locate an understandable, introductory background article for their course? In my own career I have asked each of these questions at one time or another about certain members of my own teaching faculty. The answers they give are familiar. Faculty members tell me that they know how busy I am and that they do not want to 'bother' me. I have heard from faculty that they are embarrassed about their own procrastination when it comes to course preparation. I have heard from some faculty that they had no idea academic librarians would even 'do that kind of stuff' (e.g., brainstorm assignment design or check assignments for library compatibility). While they would never admit to it, some teaching faculty feel self-conscious about not having kept up-to-date with the newest information research tools in their field.

> Unquestionably, changes in information technologies have become so common and relentless that it can be difficult even for professional librarians to keep current. Compounding this complicated situation is the fact that most new first-year students are totally unprepared to use the many complex research tools that await them in an academic library. Unfortunately, the result of these two realities can mean that a proportion of the teaching faculty will inadvertently share personal experiences with information tools that are so outmoded, that they cause serious problems for both themselves and their students. (Kohl, 1995: para. 5)

Being reluctant to look unwise in the ways of academic library research is a common, absolutely understandable reaction to today's endlessly complex information-overloaded environment. Indeed, what is most interesting about what teaching faculty say about not seeking the advice of academic librarians is that these faculty comments so closely mirror the rationalizations that their undergraduate *students* also give for not approaching a librarian for help.

Why include this particular exemplar of the potential for less-than-synergistic relationships between academic librarians and teaching faculty here? Mainly because it is a good introduction to the single most uncomplicated, least course-invasive way for teaching faculty to encourage their students' library use. Teaching faculty will always be college students' primary academic role models. Therefore, one especially undemanding way to show students the importance of an academic library is for teaching faculty to *actively model using it*. How many faculty members let their new students see them browsing in the stacks, reading quietly in the reference area or working at a library computer station every now and then? Rather than sending a student worker to pick up their own personal library resources, how many faculty members walk over and pick these materials up themselves? While it seems overly simplistic, one useful way for professors to promote information literacy is to spend some time in the library, perceptibly involved in the research process. Professors who occasionally wander through the library, greeting students and taking note of their hard work (and perhaps answering a course-related question or two), actively reinforce the library's centrality and relevance to the academic enterprise. Casually mentioning these unplanned library encounters in class is yet another great way of reinforcing student library-use and further encouraging an especially positive study habit among new undergraduates. A further way for faculty members to rather easily encourage their institutions' information literacy efforts might also be to identify and occasionally visit popular library work space(s) during a time when students are most likely to be working on a research project that they (the faculty instructor) have assigned. Taking the time to personally greet students and to ask them how their research is going is an invaluable sign that faculty expect even their newest students to be utilizing high-quality information-gathering strategies and to be diligently practicing with library research tools.

Faculty members who schedule a class meeting or two in the library, if only to orient their group to the general areas of the building that students ought to explore in relation to a particular course, begin to connect their students with valuable library tools and services in another reasonably uncomplicated way. Yet, most academic librarians realize that designating class time to work with students in the library may or may not work well with different teaching styles. While many professors are quite comfortable in today's academic library, others may feel somewhat less confident or even slightly nervous (e.g., 'What if my students ask questions about newer information technologies that I cannot answer?'). Yet, no matter how faculty choose to approach a library working day, academic librarians are eager to offer advice about, help plan for, organize and, in most cases, even to attend and/or present such sessions.

Most academic librarians find communication and collaboration with teaching faculty in this manner enormously interesting and useful. If a faculty member feels the same way about working with librarians, mentioning this fact in class is yet another painless way to reinforce the value of consulting with information professionals. By talking with students about how academic librarians assist members of the professoriate with their vocation, teaching faculty can help break down perceived barriers that might keep wary undergraduates from consulting a reference librarian. When a faculty member worries that their academic librarians are too busy to help with research or course planning (which, honestly, we rarely ever are), these faculty have an opportunity to think about and show students how best to alleviate such concerns. This is also a good teachable moment for demonstrating how a keen interest in a topic, as well as a little bit of tenacity, can help any researcher confidently approach a librarian for assistance. If a favorite librarian helps a professor with a somewhat last-minute project, the faculty member has a great example to share with students as a way of reminding them about the importance of starting research early. Using a personal procrastination example is also another particularly good way for faculty to remind students about the reliable, helpful and understanding nature of most academic librarians. If a faculty member begins to feel as though she or he is not quite current with the latest disciplinary research tools, this professor has yet another great chance to tell students how challenging effective research can be in today's information environment and also to explain the intrinsic value of consulting an academic librarian. Assuring undergraduates that librarians have good working relationships with their professors and that as a result these librarians are knowledgeable and eager to help with course-based research projects continues to advance the critically important view that today's modern academic librarians' purpose is to 'enact the learning mission of the university through being educators' (Bennett, 2009: 192).

One final point is especially important to emphasize here. Unfortunately, simply *telling* today's Millennial students to go to the reference desk and to ask for research assistance when needed is *not* an effective information literacy educational strategy. Even when professors *write down* this request in their course syllabi, most students ignore what they see as a feeble attempt at getting them to talk with old-lady librarians who then try to get students to read a bunch of time-consuming, irrelevant books. For a variety of reasons, contemporary students no longer come to reference desks with as much frequency as they once did (many do not even bother coming to the library). Therefore, merely *asking* these new Millennials to do so is simply not compelling enough for them to bother. In today's easy-Internet-access world, it has become critically important for academic librarians and teaching faculty to enthusiastically demonstrate the value and relevance of research libraries to our own lives. If we cannot clearly articulate how and provide meaningful evidence for *why* students must become effective and efficient researchers, then their dependence upon the Internet will only deepen.

Creating opportunities for close collaborations between teaching faculty and academic librarians is an important way for institutions to advance information literacy outcomes throughout their student populations. From a practical standpoint, however, working through collaborations such as these takes time, hard work and sustained effort. If collaborative first-year information literacy initiatives are to be effective, then academic librarians and teaching faculty must consider three especially important factors:

> (1) the logical and progressive development of skills and understanding in the use of information tools; (2) the appropriate relationship and counterpoint to the subject content of the student's educational development provided by the traditional professoriate; and (3) the acknowledgement of the diverse needs, and strengths, of a very complex student population. (Kohl, 1995: para. 16)

Acknowledging that an institution's newest students need to experience the library research process in stages that match their cognitive abilities, that they need to see a genuine relationship between their coursework and information literacy concepts, and that these students demonstrate a wide variety of learning styles and preferences should not inevitably translate into an 'either/or' debate when it comes to disciplinary course content. Certainly, the threat of content loss is neither an uncommon nor unreasonable faculty concern. However, academic librarians are often able to suggest ways in which the teaching of information literacy concepts can be carefully embedded into even the most rigorous of academic courses and ultimately result in a significantly positive effect on student engagement with disciplinary content. In fact, there are librarians who maintain that this entirely 'transparent' strategy helps to further privilege course content while making information literacy concepts virtually invisible to students.

> We need to move beyond the current model based on 'now the librarian is here to teach you how to become information literate in the first hour of today's class' to one in which faculty embed the building of research skills and knowledge of library resources into the course content in ways that allow students to gradually absorb it along with subject knowledge. (Miller and Bell, 2005: para. 12)

Collaborating to create courses that are rich in information literacy opportunities, such as the kind described by Miller and Bell above, need not devolve into a turf war over course content. Academic librarians recognize that disciplinary content absolutely must drive library instruction. Yet, as Miller and Bell go on to note, if the library instruction 'lacks centrality to course content, it's likely to fail' (2005: para. 13).

Academic librarians and teaching faculty must deal with the unquestionably important pedagogical issues that are tangled up with the issue of class time availability. Many of the challenges facing the information literacy movement today are due to the one-shot format into which library instruction is regularly forced. One-shots happen if a member of the teaching faculty is reluctant to collaborate too closely with a librarian or is unwilling to give up more than a limited portion of class time during which library instruction could take place. Often, these sessions necessarily seem rushed, overly ambitious and focused on passive learning pedagogies because the academic librarian ends up with a single, 50- to 70-minute session, during which he or she is forced to present a considerable amount of content. The effectiveness of the one-shot session has long been questioned by experienced librarians (Misangyi Watts, 2005: 341–2). However, after having spent almost 20 years squeezing library instruction sessions into this impracticable one-shot format, there are a few important things that I have come to understand about first-year students and their attitudes toward academic libraries.

- *Millennial students have little or no interest in academic libraries.* Most know virtually nothing about how to effectively or efficiently use one. Therefore, the only assumption teaching faculty ought to make about their first-year students' library research competence is that these novice researchers have none. While this may sound dismissive or overly dramatic, I have, on a number of occasions, heard upper-class students report, with some pride, having *never* used our institution's library. For the vast majority of new students, a library has never been an important information source.

- *First-year students will not use a large, unfamiliar, forbidding academic library strictly on their own initiative or for 'fun.'* Academic librarians and teaching faculty ceaselessly entreat new students to ask for help with their research in the library. Yet, unless they are somehow required to do so, first-year undergraduates rarely do (beyond possibly asking where the bathrooms are or how to make photocopies). When novice researchers do enter an academic library for the first time, most are anxious, overwhelmed, lost, uninterested or mainly concerned about the library's social milieu and/or campus network (Internet) access.

- *First-year students are unpracticed with effective time-management skills, especially when it comes to writing a researched paper of any length.* Unless they are intentionally led through the research process via multiple practice sessions and/or assignments scaffolded throughout a course, new students will wait until the last possible minute to begin library research. They are shocked to learn that they may not be able to complete this work in a single, last-minute library visit. They come to the library without their backpacks, a copy of their assignment, a writing utensil of any kind, paper, or their textbooks. These students assume that they can sit down, locate the perfect journal articles and/or texts in fewer than ten minutes, print their sources out and leave. Imagine their disappointment when they learn that this is a particularly poor information-gathering strategy.

- *Offering first-year students a poorly timed, single library session with no measureable outcomes is a bad idea.* Academic librarians can no more teach new students 'how to use the library' in a single class period than an experienced faculty compositionist can teach first-year undergraduates 'how to write' in that time. Due to the continuing use of one-shot library sessions as a means of delivering information literacy education, this problematic issue will be further discussed later in this book.

- *First-year students need an authentic context in which to make use of their new research competencies.* Therefore, offering a library session during the earliest weeks of a course is another bad idea. Students need to understand the context of a course before being expected to effectively apply information literacy concepts to its content. Thus, if the course requires no immediate application of newly learned research competencies to disciplinary course content, first-year students will neither retain nor transfer these concepts.

- *First-year students do not retain information literacy concepts if they are not asked to continuously practice using them.* New learners must be given enough time to apply information literacy concepts to the disciplinary content of their courses. Today's first-year students cannot passively absorb this new knowledge and then be expected to transfer it to new situations when needed (Hunt and Birks, 2004: 32). Becoming a proficient researcher requires a great deal of practice. If students are not given repeated opportunities to show what information literacy concepts they have learned, they usually forget and flounder later.

The assertions above often reveal themselves after academic librarians and teaching faculty 'try to squeeze a round peg of information literacy into some square hole in the student's mind' (Miller and Bell, 2005: para. 13). When information literacy outcomes are not intentionally or meaningfully integrated throughout a course, undergraduates quickly come to see the library as something completely external to their assignments and therefore of little value. Will improving this incorrect perception result in a change to the amount of course content that can be included in a class? To a certain extent, the answer to that question is, yes. But, not necessarily in the severe, detrimental way about which teaching faculty may initially worry. As Miller and Bell go on to describe, by working together to do away with the prevailing one-shot model, academic librarians and teaching faculty can move toward a more 'learner-centered model in which information literacy is woven into the fabric of courses, rather than added on somewhat awkwardly after the fact' (2005: para. 29). Instead of trying to clear space for a traditional one-shot library session just so a harried librarian can rush in and try to cover 'everything library' in a single course period, academic librarians and teaching faculty can integrate individual information literacy competencies and/or assignments more seamlessly into academic courses. For example, academic librarians are often able to recommend ways to merely tweak already existing coursework or suggest out-of-class homework (e.g., online tutorials, Internet-based video clips or active learning exercises) in order to include specific information literacy outcomes. Information literacy instruction could also involve abbreviated, but somewhat more frequent, librarian visits that are intentionally targeted at your students' greatest point of need. Or, information literacy competencies can be taught by teaching faculty themselves using any number of simple, active-learning techniques that do not automatically require significantly large portions of class time.

If faculty members remain concerned about having to cut large portions of disciplinary course content in order to incorporate information literacy, they might also consider the fact that many academic librarians today take a process-based approach when teaching novice researchers. As Bruce explains, 'in a process approach content is no longer paramount, but rather the ability to learn' becomes the primary focus (2004: para. 53). For academic librarians, this means that rather than lecturing ad nauseam about the fundamental library-use skills such as how to use database X, Y and Z, or how and why Boolean operators function, or where to find books in the building, etc., many of us now try to spend more time teaching larger information literacy concepts such as critical thinking and evaluation, knowledge creation and the ethics of information use. This is not to say that first-year students do not, on a certain level, need some skills-based instruction; they do. Yet, most librarians today are trying to design information literacy programs that allow our undergraduates to learn broader research concepts along a continuum similar to how they might progress within a chosen discipline. This stratified focus allows librarians to highlight research competencies that students can apply not only to their current coursework but to any future research-based project they might encounter as they progress through their academic career. According to Misangyi Watts, this instruction must go much deeper than teaching first-year students how to choose between doing a keyword search or a subject heading search.

> What we should be illuminating for students . . . is the nature of inquiry: what questions need to be asked rather than those that have already been answered. A new approach, and one to which the skills of information literacy are crucial, is a process where we teach students how to question what they know or what is known. How does one determine the best questions to ask, and how do we find questions that have not yet been asked? Students need to learn how to find answers to questions that they are interested in. (Misangyi Watts, 2005: 352)

As Misangyi Watts notes, an academic librarian's teaching depends entirely upon 'the nature of inquiry' being engendered in classrooms across our campuses. Academic librarians understand that our educational efforts are inherently interconnected with the work teaching faculty do and their students' learning experiences. Most of us are also acutely aware that we may be able to 'advise, recommend, and urge but cannot dictate or control the curriculum' (Curzon, 2004: 35). We are not interested in cheating students out of course content. However, it is also important to recognize that librarians see information literacy competency as crucial to students no matter what their discipline. Academic librarians see 'discipline-specific content skills, even when they come with critical thinking' as 'only a beginning' (Badke, 2005: 67). Most of us in the profession believe that students must, therefore, 'gain transferable strategic ability' before they can truly be considered information literate (Badke, 2005: 67). Consequently, what we want to do is help make course content, no matter the discipline, even more understandable and exciting by providing students with their own means to 'master content and extend their investigations, become more self-directed, and assume greater control over their own learning' (ACRL, 2000: 2). If academic librarians and teaching faculty can manage to balance disciplinary content and information literacy outcomes in well-planned collaborative courses, our students can only benefit by being able to reliably answer their own questions, draw better conclusions and demonstrate an enhanced understanding of the main issues within their chosen field. Curzon agrees with this important vision. She writes, 'With information literacy skills, a student's academic life is deeply enriched, their academic achievement enabled, and their capacity for lifelong learning is enhanced' (2004: 44). If we continue to focus our efforts on developing our students' critical thinking skills and the many other commonalities of purpose academic librarians and teaching faculty share, then surely innovative, successful new librarian/faculty collaborations can develop.

Students who graduate from colleges and universities today must venture out into a society that is increasingly information-based. Information literacy competency will empower these students to perform better in their courses today and allow them to practice lifelong learning tomorrow. While teaching faculty may initially have difficulty giving up class time and librarians may ask for too much class time, neither request should stop the essential conversation about how these students will gain information literacy proficiency. The benefits of this collaborative work are too great, and the consequences for not taking it on, too serious.

> What does it take? Our efforts suggest the following – more time on the design of search goals and assignments, more collaboration between faculty and librarians, and more interactions among instructors, librarians, and students. ... We all know what professors do, what librarians do, and what students do. We also know those traditional activities do not work anymore. To admit that is to enter the exciting world where instructors, students, and librarians work together to create innovations in learning. (Spence, 2004: 492)

As Spence notes above, this kind of collaborative work can be extremely rewarding. Today, the LIS literature is filled with examples of successful information literacy collaborations between academic librarians and their teaching faculty partners (Baker and Curry, 2004; Beutter, 2009; Hall, 2008; Jacobs and Jacobs, 2009; Jacobson, 2004; Pritchard, 2010; Whitehurst, 2010; etc.). It is important to note however, that many of these thriving partnerships grew slowly, progressing only after mistakes had been made and problems dealt with. It is also fair to say that the debate over disciplinary versus library course content was likely an unavoidable conversation which necessarily took place at some point during most of these collaborative efforts. Yet beyond this challenging discussion, most successful information literacy partnerships also include a shared vision between librarians and faculty, mutually agreed-upon learning outcomes, extensive ideas for curricular planning and a significant focus on meaningful assessment measures (Brasley, 2008: 74–7). Effective information literacy programs are therefore able to focus their collaborative efforts in areas where commonalities already exist and to eventually move well beyond fighting a content turf war. Such work proves that there are effective ways to create thought-provoking courses that channel valuable faculty/librarian collaboration, and effectively meet both disciplinary and information literacy outcomes.

Conclusion

Today's tech-savvy Millennial students are not impressed by stories of the long-gone halcyon days of research libraries. If first-year undergraduates are eventually going to learn from disciplinary scholarship that is both significant and trustworthy, then librarians and teaching faculty must persuade these new learners that the information literacy competencies that most of us take for granted are not 'too hard,' or 'too time-consuming,' or 'too confusing,' or, heaven forbid, 'too boring.' Unfortunately, convincing novice researchers of these things is going to take a much more comprehensive programmatic effort than has been put forth at most institutions.

> The place of the library needs to figure into the overall educational goals of any college or university. A library instruction program for first-year students must be understood in the context of the total activities of the student, the library, and the curriculum. A commitment of resources needs to be made by both, and the core intent needs to be engaging students to become information literate in both formal and informal ways. (Misangyi Watts, 2005: 344)

Research shows that, by the time they reach colleges and universities, most first-year students have integrated the

Internet into virtually every aspect of their lives. These web-savvy Millennials are likely able to locate vast amounts of Googleized information on virtually any topic. Yet, when asked to complete college-level research projects which require higher-order thinking skills such as 'interpreting, synthesizing, and creatively manipulating abstract concepts to generate new constructs, meanings, interpretations, and knowledge,' first-year students are remarkably ill-equipped for the challenge (Head and Eisenberg, 2010: 37). This is where collaborations between academic librarians and teaching faculty can be most effective. When intentionally and thoughtfully integrated throughout their first-year courses, information literacy outcomes can help novice researchers understand the need for improving upon their critical thinking and creative problem-solving skills in a variety of contexts. If academic librarians and teaching faculty provide consistent, progressively challenging research opportunities for their newest students, these novice researchers will go on to gain the kind of deep understanding for excellent, high-quality research that will ultimately initiate, sustain and extend their lifelong learning far beyond their college years (ACRL, 2000: 3).

3

Pragmatic pedagogical approaches

Abstract: This chapter offers practical advice to faculty who plan to include research projects in their work with first-year students. After briefly discussing constructivist learning theory and *Bloom's Taxonomy of Educational Outcomes*, the author suggests using an *Information Literacy Taxonomy* as a framework for developing increasingly complex library competencies among novice researchers. Additionally, the value of student-based, active learning is described and a number of guidelines for effective assignment design are provided. Finally, this chapter concludes by offering suggestions for moving information literacy beyond the first year.

Key words: novice researchers, information landscape, librarian advice, assignment design, staggered approach, faculty assumptions, topic generation, higher-order research skills, Internet, research projects, research process, outcomes, constructivist theory, Bloom's Taxonomy, Taxonomy for Information Literacy, information literacy, curricular planning, library programs, collaboration, pedagogy, active learning, faculty buy-in, semantics.

Introduction

This year, several of my favorite reference questions have been asked by students enrolled in the same first-year composition course. One of our creative young English professors commonly asks her new writing students to write a 'researched essay' which describes 'an event that you experienced or that you observed in the past.' The assignment further requires that students 'ask questions about [their event], do research to answer the questions, share the process of finding the answers, and finally, articulate the new understanding of the event or topic' (Knutson, 2010). What's more, this assignment requires new students to support their writing by locating and using 'at least two written scholarly resources' that they find using library research tools and search strategies. Based on her past experiences with this assignment, this professor has come to understand the need first-year students have for research support in the form of library instruction. Therefore, she and I have worked together for several semesters to develop a targeted library session and course webpage in an effort to teach students how to identify reliable information resources related specifically to the essay topics that they select. The students enrolled in this course usually arrive at their library session with astonishingly wide-ranging ideas for paper foci. This year was no exception. Several students wanted to explore sports-related issues. Some wanted to find information about common domestic experiences such as divorce, single parenthood or a major illness that had made an impact on their family. Other students picked topic areas such as the influence of music on learning or the value of extracurricular activities on academic performance. But my most unexpected research questions came from three young undergraduates, one of whom was working within the broad subject area of music, another, biology/physical pain, and the third . . . Well, generally speaking, I guess the third student was inspired to look into issues related to gender.

My initial conversation with the new first-year student who wanted to research music went something like this:

Student: 'I can't really find anything on my topic.'

Librarian: 'O.K. Let's see if I can help. Can you tell me a little about the topic area you are working on?'

Student: 'I want to know why I don't like music.'

Librarian: 'Oh. Well. I see. Uhm, do you mean that you want to explore why some people might not prefer a certain *type* of music? Or perhaps why certain cultures express musicality in different ways?'

Student: 'No. I just don't like music. I don't listen to it at all and I really just want to know why' (shrugs shoulders).

Thinking that this was likely to be my most challenging reference interaction with a first-year student in this particular class would have been a big mistake. Almost immediately after carefully negotiating the difficult conversation above, I encountered yet another complicated student inquiry. This second research novice's essay was certainly going to be based on personal experience. This young woman planned to further explore her experience with a large tattoo she had recently acquired on her lower back. As this novice researcher eagerly explained her ideas for the composition to me, it became clear that what she really wanted to investigate was why it hurt so much more to have the tattoo applied to one side of her back than it did to have it applied to the other side.

The final unanticipated question asked by a new student in this class came from a fairly brash young woman. When I asked her what she was interested in researching, this first-year student loudly announced that she was going to write her academic essay on why young men are so attracted to female breasts.

Beyond the express amusement each of these topic ideas forced me to conceal, their intellectual naiveté still leaves me almost speechless. Yet, Head and Eisenberg's recent publication, *Truth Be Told: How College Students Evaluate and Use Information in the Digital Age* (2010), sheds some light on what is likely happening to these painfully inexperienced new college undergraduates. According to these authors, most students actually report having quite a lot of course-related questions that they would like to further explore through research. Indeed, this is true in the case of the three undergraduates noted above. Despite a complete lack of scholarly significance, their entirely open-ended (unanswerable) design and the absence of any real disciplinary research potential, at a bare minimum, these three students' questions do meet their instructor's assignment criterion. Most importantly, these young students are actively engaging with what they each believe is a fascinating topic idea. However, what is also likely happening to these novice researchers is that they are being asked to do the kind of academic research which initiates 'a process few students thoroughly understand and grasp with much confidence' (Head and Eisenberg, 2010: 33). In fact, Head and Eisenberg's study found that

> getting started in the course-related research process stymied a large majority of students in the sample (84 percent) more than any other step in their research

process. Other significant challenges occurred toward the beginning of the research process, too, including defining a topic (66 percent), narrowing it down (62 percent), and sorting through search results to find relevant materials (61 percent). (Head and Eisenberg, 2010: 26)

These authors go on to say that 'students' biggest difficulties were in determining the nature and scope of a research assignment and what it required of them' (Head and Eisenberg, 2010: 36). Clearly the three first-year undergraduates described above are unprepared to ask the kind of questions that translate well into manageable, researchable, academic essay topics. Additionally, due to their lack of disciplinary background, none realize that they might be able to draw upon a larger body of work that might inspire improved research possibilities. Asking meaningful research questions requires, at a minimum, *some* basic understanding of a topic area and the way in which individual disciplines might approach that topic. This means that some external reading about a topic and the discipline in which it falls is often essential (especially for first-year students) to do *before* trying to develop effective research questions.

Creating authentic research-based assignments, the kinds that include explicit instructions and carefully thought-out information literacy outcomes (especially for those students who are newest to the academy), is a critical step toward boosting student success. Also, improving students' ability to efficiently and effectively locate high-quality sources of information can only have a positive impact upon how new undergraduates learn from *any* assignment that requires reading beyond their course-assigned texts. As Orme writes, unless the tenets of information literacy are 'explicitly addressed as part of a first-year curriculum' and students provided 'the necessary mechanics and resources attendant in a university setting,' the kind of 'lifelong learning that information literacy advocates have promised' will be unlikely to take hold (Orme, 2008: 70). How, then, might academic librarians and teaching faculty together relinquish outmoded approaches to the research library and move toward information literacy theories and instructional pedagogies which are authentic, student-centered and successful? In other words, how can library supporters at academic institutions collaborate to make information literacy competency a central focus 'so that skills are taught and developed in context, and students can apply the learning to real situations' (Hunt and Birks, 2004: 30)?

One of the most basic steps to take is to develop an appreciation for the sheer scope and complexity of the information landscape with which neophyte researchers must currently cope. The following is a single example of the type of statistical breakdown which often appears as a result of today's overwhelming research environment. What may be most interesting about the subsequent quotation is that by the time this book is published, this data will likely be noticeably out of date.

> 'Information' is growing at a compound annual rate of 60 percent. The amount of electronic data produced by computers, cameras, recorders, and the like surpassed the capacity of storage technologies back in 2007 (at about 250 exabytes). One current estimate of total global information production is 1.2 zettabytes. Only 5 percent of the information that is created is 'structured,' i.e., in a standard format of words or numbers that can be read by humans or computers. (Pattillo, 2010: 276)

Despite the fleeting validity of quantitative analyses such as the one above, the fact remains that today's information-saturated environment is remarkably different than it was even five short years ago. While those of us who are digital non-natives may wish to turn back the clock on the myriad of ways information is currently being shared, for our students' sakes, we cannot. As Misangyi Watts cautions, 'Information literacy is a nexus for the life experiences of the student, the academic world of scholarship and the postcollege [*sic*] real world of application of learning' (2005: 348). It is, therefore, important to remember that hearkening back to nostalgic, past library experiences has little if any relevance to today's Millennial undergraduates. These are students who increasingly have never visited a public library and have rarely had access to, much less any meaningful experience with, high-quality middle- or high-school libraries. As many academic librarians will attest,

> Gone are the days of the library research marathon during which the student spent hours tracking down the available documents, filling out interlibrary loan requests, and reading in the rare books room. The concept of an assignment that could take an entire semester to complete is outside the realm of most students' understanding. The treasure-hunt approach to research and the satisfaction of finding the research treasure are long gone. (Burkhardt et al., 2003: ix)

Today's library information tools and search processes display little if any resemblance to the antiquated scenario described above. With the advent of the Internet and the astonishing speed with which information technology has expanded, students today are faced with significantly more complex research options than past students ever were. Upon receiving even the most carefully designed research assignments, contemporary undergraduates are asked to make sense out of an enormous array of easily available information choices. And, as Head and Eisenberg assert, not only do these novice researchers have to worry about trying to use their new research library, these students 'grapple with what college-level research assignments mean and what is expected of them in the process of intellectual discovery' (2010: 36). As a result of the rapidly increasing complexity of today's information landscape, as well as what we know about the variability in our first-year students' cognitive abilities, it is no longer enough for teaching faculty to assume their students will ask a librarian for help when needed or that these new students will be able to figure out how the library works on their own. Head and Eisenberg go on to suggest that 'Faculty need to think carefully about the learning goals and means of their assignments – beyond subject or content – and focus on substantively helping students to learn and practice research skills' (2010: 39). Unfortunately, if a professor portrays the academic research library as a staid, print-bound knowledge repository or, worse, if he or she ignores it altogether, students are left to flounder about as best as they can in order to complete their research projects. Usually, this means making use of the one information tool with which they are most familiar but least discerning about – the Internet.

Fortunately, as this book has already noted, neither teaching faculty nor academic librarians need to undertake the work of incorporating information literacy competencies into their undergraduate researchers' learning experiences alone. As Rockman reminds her readers, there are already many examples of thriving faculty/librarian collaborations 'focused on research strategies, the expanding pedagogical use of information resources, and the importance of developing creative, open-ended assignments as a means for teaching [and embedding] information literacy skills in the curriculum' (2004a: 241). Getting first-year students, such as the three described at the beginning of this chapter, from the point of investigative naiveté at which they begin their college careers to the point at which they can successfully 'use the cognitive activities of defining a topic and narrowing it down' is a task best done as a result of academic librarians and teaching faculty working together (Head and Eisenberg, 2010: 39). Today, a wide array of collaborative strategies exist for teaching faculty and academic librarians who would like to work together in support of their first-year students' research competencies. The following chapter highlights a number of these innovative approaches and also serves as a framework for those teaching faculty who wish to further explore effective research assignment design and information literacy assessment.

From the start: advice from librarian colleagues

Teaching faculty should not be afraid to start small when considering how best to collaborate with an academic librarian and/or incorporate information literacy into a first-year academic course. At my own institution, some of the most successful faculty/librarian collaborations have developed after very humble beginnings. Here, librarians have cultivated good working relationships with teaching faculty as a result of research assignments that unfortunately went awry, participating in professional development opportunities, leading a segment of new faculty orientation and, often, simply through word of mouth. Currently, one of my favorite collaborations is with a language professor, who for years has been extremely receptive to and wonderfully supportive of our library's emphasis on information literacy competency. What I enjoy most about working with this member of our faculty is that she is amazingly flexible in terms of how our collaboration continues to develop over time. When she and I first began working together I would often appear in her classrooms for several hurried and harried library sessions. At that time the library at our institution did not have a particularly effective teaching space and so I had to regularly take the library show on the road. As a result I was often unable to do much more than demonstration and lecture-style presentations, which I imagined might not only put off the poor language students, but their professor as well. Yet, this faculty member stuck with me. We have continued to talk about her concern at how unprepared students are to do academic research in the English language, much less their capacity for doing it in another language, and together we have negotiated a number of effective ways to further educate and support these novice researchers. Over the years this faculty member and I have been willing to try different pedagogical approaches. My presentations have certainly improved, as have the research assignments this faculty member now asks her students to complete. (Though I should note that the single most important requirement – locating, evaluating and using high-quality information sources produced *in the language of the course* – remains.) Certainly, not every strategy we have tried has been equally as successful. But we continue to learn a great deal from the work we do together and what is most rewarding is that our students benefit considerably from the genuine information literacy learning opportunities these courses now provide.

When discussing a newly conceived library-based research project with faculty members who are teaching first-year courses, I usually begin with two key pieces of advice: 1) try very hard not to make even small assumptions about new undergraduates' purported library research skills; and 2) help new students tackle the research process using some type of logical and staged project framework. Of these two suggestions, the first, the appeal not to assume anything about first-year students' library research skills, is the one with which I see teaching faculty struggle most often. It is my hope that the brief accounts of my past experiences with novice researchers which appear throughout this book will serve as a gentle caution to teaching faculty in this regard. Amusing as they may appear on the surface, these stories clearly illustrate the depth of most first-year students' vacuity when it comes to doing the work of academic research. However, rather than providing reference desk entertainment, such interactions are often complicated, demanding and prolonged. Speculation about the extent to which Millennial students possess library competencies (or have any interest in possessing them) time and again results in anxiety, frustration and disappointment for teaching faculty, academic librarians and newly matriculating undergraduates. Spence, a university composition instructor, describes just such an experience after having tried to assign research assignments to his students based on his own personal belief that library research is 'passionate, free, and exhilarating' (2004: 486).

> Time-harried, yet wasteful, students collected far more information than they needed or could understand. They mucked about without a guiding question, filling folders and floppy disks with notes and citations patched into sprawling papers difficult to read or critique. All-nighters produced piles, which, at best, were raw drafts of some background of a possibly interesting idea followed by brief suggestions for further research. (Spence, 2004: 487)

Regrettably, even those students who did poorly on Spence's assignment *insisted* that they already knew how to use a library. Even more worrying is the negative response with which an academic librarian's initial attempt at library instruction to this group was met. As this book has already explained, first-year students commonly report having a great deal of confidence in their research abilities (Gross and Latham, 2009: 345–7). Yet, new undergrads seldom have any experience with the kind of scholarly sources, academic research tools or search strategies that they need to successfully complete college-level work. As Lippincott writes, today's Millennials

> come to campus having played hours of video games, having spent much of their spare time surfing the Net and instant messaging their friends, and having used multiple electronic devices simultaneously. [Yet] . . . we [continue to] hear complaints from faculty that [these] students use inappropriate sources from the Web to support their ideas in term papers instead of peer-reviewed academic resources; that they submit multimedia projects that are superficial and full of glitz, not substance – and that they no longer read, period. (Lippincott, 2005: 13.6)

It may be helpful to repeat that, for most new undergraduates, the Internet *is* the library. New students can find scads of information about virtually any topic using the Internet. Yet, they still struggle with higher-level information literacy competencies such as generating researchable topics that are interesting and intellectually appropriate. Further, when it comes to focusing the broad topic ideas they do have by asking germane, consequential research questions, these novices need considerable support with this process from faculty and librarians. The literature of library and information science (LIS) is clear about this seemingly contradictory phenomenon. Studies show that though they insist that they already know how to do research, a significant number of incoming undergraduates have 'little or no idea how to choose, define, and limit the scope of a topic' (Head and Eisenberg, 2009: 6).

The second piece of advice that I usually offer professors is that they should try to ensure that their newest students have an opportunity to start at the very beginning of the research process and to engage with this entire process at a reasonable pace. This is not to say that research should be presented to new students as a rigid, linear process. As most expert researchers know, the research process is recursive, flexible and, to a certain extent, personal. Yet, brand-new first-year students have had few if any opportunities to develop a complete picture of what the research process might actually entail. Initially, their main priority is likely to be increasing the expediency with which they can complete their research process. These students regularly skip as many stages of research as they possibly can by going straight to the Internet. Very few will have had experience with strategies such as concept mapping (brainstorming), reading valuable reference sources (gaining insight into a subject area) or using more than one type of information source (books, book chapters, journal articles, newspapers, government publications, etc.). Academic librarians and teaching faculty need to work together to show students why adding such phases to their research process is important.

One idea to keep in mind is that research projects often work especially well for novice researchers when they are carefully staged or broken up into smaller, more manageable phases across a portion of the course.

> Without a sense of process, students have difficulty recognizing similarities in circumstances necessary for transferring skills from one situation to another. The central goal of information literacy is to instill in students a sense of the process of learning from a variety of sources of information and skills to construct their own understandings from that information. (Kuhlthau, 2004: 164)

Unfortunately, if first-year students are given the opportunity to avoid practicing any element of the research process they will do so to save time. As Spence quickly learned, if new undergraduates are merely presented with a research project description (even a description that is carefully written) and left to their own devices, their final projects will likely reflect an emphasis on efficacy rather than content. In addition, their ability to transfer any meaningful knowledge about the research process will be lost when it comes to completing their next library-based assignment.

When designing a research project for novice researchers, teaching faculty should first carefully consider and then target certain information literacy outcomes. Start by asking which information literacy competencies are *most* important for students to be able to demonstrate as a result of having completed the research assignment. At a very basic level, teaching faculty might ask whether or not their new students most need to know how to identify, locate and check out library books that are interesting and relevant to their courses. Perhaps it is more important that these students are able to identify different information types and understand when each is most appropriately used (reference books, general collection items, periodicals, newspapers, government publications, etc.). Or, faculty members might want to prioritize their students' ability to understand and effectively use a particular periodical index. Whichever information literacy outcomes teaching faculty select must be made explicit to first-year students. These students can then be held accountable for demonstrating mastery of each outcome as a result of having completed their research project.

If identifying suitable information literacy outcomes seems too complicated or time-consuming, teaching faculty might consult ACRL's *Information Literacy Competency Standards for Higher Education* (ACRL, 2000). Available online (see the reference list at the end of this book for the URL), this extensive list is a great way to begin thinking about a variety of outcomes and how they might be integrated into library-based research assignments. A note of caution: faculty should not let the length or detail of this document deter them. The *Standards* are intended to be a malleable tool which can help academic librarians and teaching faculty to think collaboratively about the many dimensions of information literacy competency. The *Standards* also serve as a framework for ways in which these competencies might be more clearly articulated and taught as a part of an entire college curriculum. The performance indicators and outcomes listed in the *Standards* document should absolutely be molded and shaped to fit individual assignments, courses or curricula. Obviously, teaching faculty should not expect to incorporate every information literacy outcome into every assignment or course. Rather, a good strategy is to start by examining the *Standards* and considering how an assignment might, even in its earliest form, incorporate aspects of information literacy competency. Once several relevant competencies have been identified, teaching faculty can ask, 'Which of these outcomes are *most* important for students to master so that they can successfully complete this research project?' (Unless a faculty member and librarian are actually co-teaching the course, I often suggest selecting four or fewer for first-year students.)

113

Once the central information literacy outcomes have been identified, clearly state them in a syllabus, on the assignment description or in both places for students as a way of reinforcing their importance.

Perhaps the most helpful advice for selecting information literacy outcomes for any first-year research project is to remember that less is definitely more. Students need to be allowed enough time to practice and master these new strategies, so that rather than using the 'dump truck method,' where professors or academic librarians overwhelm students 'with more skills and strategies than they can possibly absorb,' a professor might select two or three key objectives and offer students a variety of opportunities to practice and internalize them (qtd. in Keyser, 2000: 37). It is also important to note that academic librarians are especially eager to help teaching faculty identify suitable information literacy outcomes. Librarians have an interesting perspective on the research process and the expertise to help faculty think about, identify and seamlessly incorporate information literacy outcomes into virtually any research-based assignment.

The timing of each phase of a research project is another aspect to carefully consider. Professors need to bear in mind the multiplicity of research difficulties facing their newest students. Even small inconveniences can have a significant impact on a neophyte researcher's ability and/or willingness to satisfactorily complete a project. For example, teaching faculty might want to consider that first-year undergraduates often need as much support learning how to physically *find* books in an academic library building (assuming their research project requires consulting an academic text or two) as they do negotiating a thesis statement. Upon entering their new research facilities, first-year college students soon find that even the numbers on the book spines look different from those they may have seen before. Finding books for the first time, then, especially in a large university setting, can be an extremely anxiety-provoking, excruciatingly time-consuming activity for brand-new undergrads. Such students commonly believe that they should be able to easily and quickly locate their items. If this turns out not to be the case, they are often too embarrassed to ask for assistance. If permitted, this is one activity most novice researchers will eagerly avoid by using the Internet. For scores of first-year undergrads, finding books in a large academic library is a tricky, completely new component of their research process, one to which very few expert researchers give a second thought.

Certainly, I am not suggesting that teaching faculty designate entire class periods to having students examine and memorize the minutiae of LCC. Nevertheless, being aware of how difficult it can be for first-year students to locate materials among scores of library stacks might make offering a quick practice session (possibly using an older, library-savvy peer mentor) early in the course worthwhile. This knowledge might also prompt a quick library resource check with undergraduates early in the project. Students could be asked to bring in a library item and briefly describe how it will influence their final project. At a minimum, knowing how first-year students struggle to locate library materials might also be a good factor to consider when setting due dates for certain portions of the overall project.

Guidance of the kind offered here is the result of many years of experience gained after working alongside countless stressed-out undergraduate researchers. Increasingly, however, this type of experience-based advice is being further informed by what educational theorists today describe as constructivist-based learning. Constructivist theory suggests that learners build knowledge and skills upon their already-existing constructs of the world based upon individual experience. Constructivist theory contends that the learner brings to the learning environment knowledge from past experience, and that knowledge has a strong influence upon how the learner constructs meaning and acquires new knowledge from new experiences. Additionally, advocates of constructivist approaches believe that the process of knowledge acquisition and creation, in order to become stored in long-term memory, must be active rather than passive, and must also be applicable to the learner's everyday world and experiences. (Allen, 2008: 30–1)

In the case of brand-new undergraduates, it may be true that they come to their colleges and universities having had *some* type of experience with whatever constituted research at their local high schools or perhaps even a local public library. As Malcolm Brown quips, no learners 'come to a classroom . . . with a mind that is a tabula rasa, a blank slate' (2005: 12.4). Yet, as librarians well know, there is no consensus among secondary school educators about what the term 'research' actually means and, as a result, it is *broadly* defined by a multitude of individual high-school educators. Furthermore, as this book has already pointed out, funding for school libraries and the qualified personnel who operate them continues to rapidly disappear from many American school district budgets, leaving more and more students with no access to the kind of resources that might help them more easily transition to college-level research.

Sadly, the fact that most first-year students have had little or no previous experience with the type of library-based research tools or investigative strategies that college professors and over-eager academic librarians might expect must, yet again, be reiterated. Burkhardt, MacDonald and Rathemacher have found that first-year students often do not 'know how the library materials available electronically are different from those they find surfing the Web. Some students have never learned [how] to use a periodical database or an on-line catalog' (2003: x). Compounding their lack of experience with academically rigorous research sources and techniques is the reality that first-year students come to their institutions 'at varying levels of cognitive development,' which means that some of them are simply not intellectually 'ready to seek information with high levels of reflective and critical thinking' (Weiler, 2004: 51–2). As Barbara Valentine and Steven Bernhisel confirm,

> High school students still come to college with varied levels of critical awareness, information savvy, and technological experience. They still need to learn the difference between academic and popular literature and thought. More than ever they need to learn to seek context and history in order to think critically about what they find. (2008: 511)

Leamnson acknowledges the cognitive variance among first-year students by writing, 'There is little danger in overestimating the intellectual potential of our students, but there is serious danger in overestimating the conditions of their brains' (2003: 15). Further, according to this author, today's first-year students often do not recognize their own inexperience, and the confidence so many of them display 'stems from the mistaken belief that there is nothing really new here [i.e., in college]' (Leamnson, 2003: 36).

Without a doubt, similar misconceptions pertain to the academic library. In fact, new students often appear at our desks with ideas about research that need to be *un*learned. For example, one new student with whom I recently worked told me that he could not believe how nice the librarians at our institution were because his high-school library 'basically consisted of one shelf of *Harlequin* romances and a bitter old woman.' Is it really any surprise that novice researchers such as this young man need so much guidance and support when it comes to locating, evaluating and using high-quality, college-level information sources?

In addition to encouraging faculty members to examine information literacy education through a constructivist lens, academic librarians at my institution also urge teaching faculty to keep a version of *Bloom's Taxonomy of Educational Objectives* in mind. Using *Bloom's* as a framework is one excellent way to visualize a potential structure for information literacy competencies throughout individual courses, as well as entire disciplinary majors. At my institution librarians have modified *Bloom's* into a progressive taxonomy for information literacy. This diagram has been a particularly effective way to illustrate how increasingly more sophisticated research proficiencies might fit into various courses, majors or even the colleges' core curriculum (see Figure 3.1).

My librarian colleagues and I use this heuristic for two main purposes. First, we want to visually prompt teaching faculty to recognize the need for starting their newest students out with what may seem, to expert researchers, like extremely simple library usage skills. These aptitudes relate to learning necessary research/library terminology, exploring useful service areas, understanding the library's policies and procedures, recognizing various library organizational modes, being able to identify various information source types, etc., as identified at the bottom of the information literacy staircase.

Figure 3.1 Taxonomy for information literacy

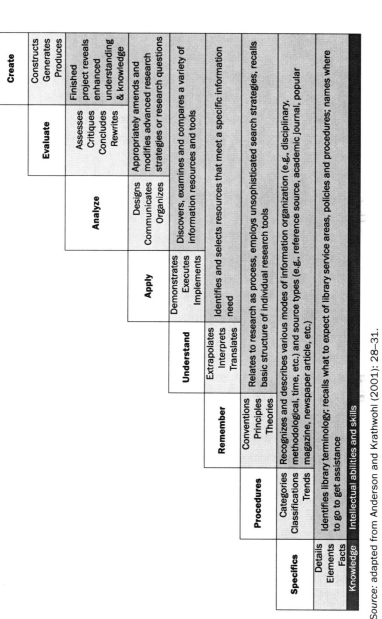

Source: adapted from Anderson and Krathwohl (2001): 28–31.

To achieve information literacy goals successfully, instructors must first break down the skills and concepts into their basic components – deconstructing what they may (or may not) do, without consciously thinking about it, into the smaller incremental steps and concepts that students need to learn. These components should then be presented sequentially and in increasing levels of complexity, allowing time for practice and repetition. (Hunt and Birks, 2004: 28)

As this author has already observed, many teaching faculty persist in being overly optimistic about their first-year students' library research abilities. Studies continue to show that professors often 'expect their students to know how to find research materials without ever teaching these skills or having any clear idea of how students are supposed to learn them' (Foster and Gibbons, 2007: 4). Yet, new students come to college with little if any sense of how libraries are structured, unable to comprehend most basic library terminology (e.g., reference, circulation, reserve, periodical, etc.), not knowing where to ask for help and unable to name even the most basic of services offered by their campus library. One study found that 'Thirty-two percent of college student respondents are not sure that their libraries offer electronic journals. Thirty-one percent are not sure that their libraries provide online databases. Twenty-three percent are not sure if their libraries have online reference materials' (OCLC, 2006: 3–24). Because these incoming undergraduates are so inexperienced with even the most elementary of library skills, asking them to complete research assignments that require proficiencies at the higher end of the information literacy taxonomy is likely to be an exercise in frustration. Before they can effectively analyze, evaluate and create new information, first-year students must build their information literacy competency from the bottom up. This is why something as simple as urging new students to ask a reference librarian for research help may be a pointless exercise. Many first-year students do not recognize the term 'reference,' have no idea (or worse, the wrong idea) about what a librarian does and are just as unlikely to know where such library-types might actually hang out.

One analogy that I like to make as a way of further illustrating the benefits of starting today's first-year students at the bottom of the information literacy taxonomy is to invite faculty to think back to their own dissertation-writing days. I ask these professors to consider the methods by which they were taught how to write a dissertation. I then remind faculty that they may not have even known what a dissertation *was* as a first-year undergraduate. During this discussion, teaching faculty quickly acknowledge that it took *years* of academic preparation before they were able to research and write a manuscript of such depth. I typically ask faculty to remember that new students must first master all of the research skills that are required of them in order to generate a high-quality researched essay, long before they ever consider writing a dissertation. They cannot do this if they are randomly skipping around the information literacy taxonomy.

Though it is greatly oversimplified, this analogy reinforces the idea that becoming information literate is likely to be a lengthy if not lifelong process. This is also a process that requires mastery of many research abilities which must continually build upon one another. When students are asked to skip important building-block skills, such as learning how to effectively use the library's online catalog, initiate interlibrary loans or identify the differences between a library database and freely available Internet resources, their ability to move to the next level of information literacy is often further complicated by increasing library anxiety and/or an increasing lack of motivation (i.e., 'Everything I need is on the Internet. Why bother with the library?').

Not only does the dissertation analogy advance the suggestion that starting new students at the beginning of the academic research process is essential, it also highlights a second significant use of the information literacy taxonomy, which is to show the value of carefully structuring information literacy opportunities. As Weiler observes, new undergraduates 'must go through a series of steps over a period of time before they are able to seek information critically and reflectively' (2004: 52). Kuh et al. agree, further explaining:

> First-year students must first master the foundational skills of distinguishing between types of information sources, formulating search queries, and using reference sources [in any format] before acquiring more complex research competencies such as evaluating resources and using discipline-specific materials. (2007: 23)

For all practical purposes, teaching students to be information literate involves the same type of educational progression as learning to write a dissertation. This analogy allows for a number of comparisons that should resonate especially well with faculty who have gone through the process of writing their dissertation. For example, new student learners should not skip haphazardly through a 'piecemeal implementation of library instruction' (Kohl, 1995: para. 2). Simply taking a tour of the library will no more make a first-year student information literate than showing that same student where the finished dissertations are kept would prepare that student to write one. Attempting to teach a brand-new undergraduate 'how to use' today's modern library in a single fifty-minute instruction session would no more make that student information literate than spending the same amount of time talking about the process of researching and writing a dissertation would prepare that student to complete one. First-year students can no more write a dissertation after a single semester of college than they can efficiently or effectively navigate through the massive amounts of information currently being hurled at them via the Internet.

If academic librarians and teaching faculty want information literacy competency to be important to contemporary Millennial undergraduates, 'library instruction must be planned strategically across the curriculum and implemented in a way that allows the student to grasp the complexities of the information universe' (Nerz and Weiner, 2001: para. 30). Today's first-year undergraduates need 'a logical focused progression of instruction in the use of modern information tools,' and yet, instilling the notion that information literacy education is an essential, developmentally based, ongoing progression has not been easy (Kohl, 1995: para. 16).

> What becomes lost in the choppy, incidental instruction [students] receive in various courses is an awareness of the process. If students have no concept of how the information universe is structured, if they cannot use 'traditional library tools,' and if they have never had to solve an information problem using an appropriate research method, then they will not be competent acquirers, users, managers, and transformers of information. (Nerz and Weiner, 2001: para. 18)

Moving first-year information literacy programming beyond the kind of 'choppy, incidental instruction' described by Nerz and Weiner has been an ongoing challenge at many institutions, my own included. While we have made a great deal of progress at this institution, faculty holdouts do remain. These few professors seem to have difficulty subscribing to the idea that information literacy programming is worth what they see as a direct trade-off in terms of more important course content. Various faculty members also believe that peer-led library tours given to all of the college's incoming first-year students during their general orientation are ineffective. And though librarians carefully crafted this opportunity as a way to further reinforce and extend a peer-led tour experience, some of our faculty also take issue with an active learning exercise currently required of all new undergraduates enrolled in the college's first-year seminar. While the outcomes for both of these introductory library experiences are admittedly modest (students are introduced to the building, our staff, a general online periodical index, a reference source, the reserve collection, a multistep printing system and the print periodical collection), neither the peer-led tour nor the active learning exercise is meant to be completed out of order or in isolation from one another. Nor are these activities intended to produce completely information-literate students. However, when new students participate in both opportunities, librarians report positive results, particularly related to our students' confidence and their willingness to try new research strategies and library tools. We also notice a change in the depth of reference questions answered at the reference desk. Rather than dealing with hundreds of logistical/directional questions at the beginning of each new academic year, librarians now seem to focus more on questions related to specific research projects, library tools or search strategies. Teaching faculty, especially those who have their first-year students complete both initial library experiences and then also follow up with a third or even fourth library session, invariably report improvements to their new students' research-based projects, especially when compared to projects completed by students who skipped their orientation tour and/or active learning exercise. While it is true that library tours and simple, experiential activities alone will not immediately produce spectacularly information-literate first-year students, it is also true that these novice researchers have no context whatsoever for library use. By starting at the very beginning of our information literacy taxonomy, librarians at this institution hope that our newest students' earliest experiences in an academic library are positive and successful rather than opportunities for building frustration and fear.

Another thing that I often talk about with first-year teaching faculty is my conviction that the more directly academic librarians and teaching faculty work together, the more likely it is that our newest students will benefit from research experiences that are both meaningful and lasting. According to ACRL's *Standards*, 'Achieving competency in information literacy requires an understanding that this cluster of abilities is not extraneous to the curriculum but is woven into the curriculum's content, structure, and sequence' (ACRL, 2000: 5). Though it seems obvious, if academic librarians and teaching faculty hope to develop this understanding further, both groups need to do a better job of talking with one another (Birmingham et al., 2008; Fister, 1995). According to Hunt and Birks, close collaboration between teaching faculty and librarians 'is essential for best practices in information literacy instruction and cannot be considered in isolation' (2004: 31). These authors go on to elaborate by noting that working together often serves a variety of functions. According to them, collaborative work 'fosters the sharing of ideas, expertise, and provides opportunities for exposure to different pedagogies, as well as new teaching/learning techniques. It also enables colleagues to become familiar with each other's fields' (31). Working together is also critically important because today's techno-savvy Millennials are likely to take information literacy seriously *only* if they see that the quality of their research work is integrally related to project successes or failures in college and/or their professional lives after college.

Most academic librarians eagerly welcome collaborative work. I truly enjoy suggesting innovative strategies that might help teaching faculty more seamlessly integrate information literacy competencies into a specific research assignment or course. Visiting with an academic librarian about a new course, preparing a rough draft of the course syllabus together or collaboratively planning out several staggered research assignments are all great ways to ensure that first-year students do not view library instruction as something separate from course content and thus, yet another meaningless hoop to jump through. In fact, this is precisely the kind of communication that is vital to the success of advancing information literacy competency as an overarching undergraduate educational outcome.

> Working together and pooling their perspectives and knowledge, librarians and first-year classroom faculty can do more to create positive library experiences and ensure students' success than either group working separately. Frequent and good communication is the key to a positive library experience in the first year. (Hardesty, 2007: 116)

The importance of engaging in frequent dialog with one another cannot be overstated. If librarians do not fully understand the primary goals or structure of an academic course, they may be hard-pressed to offer the kind of integrated research assistance that Millennial students see as worthwhile. If teaching faculty misunderstand the significance of selecting appropriate information literacy outcomes or the value of staging their first-year students' research projects over time, they may resent an academic librarian's seemingly off-target presentation and, in the end, remain discouraged by their students' research capabilities (Spence, 2004: 491–2). Worst, if there is poor, infrequent communication between academic librarians and their teaching faculty, the fall-back option is more likely to be the vague, one-shot 'how to library' session which has little if any consequential impact on student learning. Proactively talking about, planning for and structuring a course-based research assignment together while utilizing one another's expertise is simply the best way to ensure that novice researchers are fully supported during their most formative library experiences.

Creating effective library experiences

If there is one noticeably different generational feature of today's new college students, it is the increasing emphasis these students place on speed and ease. Bruce Harley refers to this focus as 'the postmodern condition' (2001: 302). He goes on to cite another of his own articles written with two additional authors (Dreger and Knobloch) as a way of further describing the characteristics of this condition as a 'preference for the convenient and expedient, and emphasis on outward appearances and a reliance on subjective thinking' (qtd. in Harley, 2001: 302). This attitudinal shift has increased the pressure, particularly on our newest students, to subvert as much of the academic research process as possible in the interest of time. Today's first-year undergraduates are completely 'product focused rather than process focused' (Nerz and Weiner, 2001: para. 7). So much so, that I regularly find myself reminding them that in order to successfully complete an academic research project they have to invest the necessary amount of time it takes to actually *read* and process their information resources. For many contemporary undergraduates the idea of assiduously exploring a research question and learning something new is not nearly as important as 'getting the assignment completed and turned in' (Nerz and Weiner, 2001: para. 7). Additionally, because these new students may not yet possess the higher-level cognitive skills necessary to effectively reflect upon and analyze their sources, the likelihood of their being able to create something much beyond a report-level response is slight (Hardesty, 2007: 110–11). Commonplace first-year information literacy shortcomings such as these create major pedagogical dilemmas for academic librarians and teaching faculty. As Hardesty remarks, 'as we challenge first-year students to develop their information literacy skills, we risk some students becoming frustrated and forming long-lasting, negative attitudes towards the library and the research process' (2007: 111). If this is the case, then what might librarians and members of the teaching faculty do to avoid 'creating library assignments [that function] as add-ons to courses' and further promote 'student hostility' to the entire research process (Spence, 2004: 491)?

Early in his chapter on teaching and pedagogy Leamnson writes, 'Telling students what they need to know is one thing; *doing* something that will inspire them to become motivated and actually learn is quite another' (Leamnson, 2003: 55). Though his insinuation about the shortcomings of the traditional lecture format is well taken, supporters of constructivist learning theory might more fully appreciate this sentiment if Leamnson had instead suggested that his *students* need to be more actively involved in 'doing something' that motivates and fosters their learning. Rather than focusing on teaching faculty as the primary agents responsible for student learning, constructivism puts the focus back on learners. In a constructivist setting, instructors function more as guides or facilitators while students proceed through active learning exercises that help them to contextualize and process new information.

Academic libraries provide an ideal learning environment in which teaching faculty might make use of a variety of student-centered learning pedagogies. The following active-learning pedagogical strategies can work especially well in an academic library setting:

- *Cognitive apprenticeships* – This strategy might be developed by an expert researcher who uses techniques such as modeling or coaching to guide teams of novice researchers through the completion of a complex library project or research-based problem.

- *Communities of practice (CoP)* – This strategy can be used when expert researchers ask their novice researchers to take part in the process that ensues when people with a common interest collaborate over time to share ideas, solve problems and seek new ways of thinking. Asking student groups to examine an intriguing question of shared appeal and to then present their solutions through creative oral/visual presentations, multifaceted panel discussions or even a professional-grade annotated bibliography, etc., are all good options for anchoring CoP activities in an academic research library.

- *Discovery learning* – This strategy involves creating a problem-solving situation where student learners draw on their own past experiences and existing knowledge to discover new facts, relationships and information. At my institution, librarians successfully employ this inquiry-based method as a way of introducing brand-new students to important service areas and basic research tools. Theme-based handouts are given to pairs of first-year undergrads, who explore the library building while answering a number of intentionally open-ended questions. While these students are encouraged to ask for help when they need it, they are mainly asked to complete their questionnaires by building upon their own past, albeit limited, experience with libraries.

- *Goal-based scenarios (GBS)* – Another excellent form of hands-on learning, GBS focus on a specific set of required skills, the demonstration of which is seamlessly integrated into a high student-interest activity. This method can function quite naturally in the college library. The key to using this technique in an academic library is to first carefully identify the specific research skills (information literacy concepts) students must acquire. Once target skills have been identified, teaching faculty and academic librarians can collaboratively use their expertise to create the kind of high student-interest, course-related topical scenarios that really motivate undergraduates.

- *Problem-based learning (PBL)* – This instructional method has been used in academic libraries for some time (Nugent and Myers, 2000; Carder et al., 2001; Spackman and Camacho, 2009). The basic premise is that student learning should be the result of having actively wrangled with messy, real-world problems. Academic librarians are eager to support teaching faculty who use this teaching strategy as another way to involve students in research projects that are especially compelling. The keys to effectively using this pedagogy in the library are close collaboration between teaching faculty and librarians and the identification of specific information literacy outcomes that students should master as a result of having taken part in the problem-solving process.

- *Situated learning* – This pedagogical strategy is easily supported by academic libraries. One especially effective way for novice researchers to learn how to do academic research is to simply immerse them in the environment where they must complete this work. Logically then, first-year students need to spend some time actually working in their college or university library. Most contemporary academic libraries have at least one or two learning spaces which allow students to experience the library as a classroom. At my institution quite a number of teaching faculty arrange for 'research days' with their first-year students. These class periods are reserved so that students can engage in the 'authentic activity, context, and culture' of their college library. A word of caution about this strategy. It is *not* enough to bring brand-new students into the library and say, 'Get to work.' These sessions work well only if: a) novice researchers have had at least one or two previous library sessions to prepare them for this work, and b) the professor gives her students specific, library outcomes for the session. For example an instructor might say, 'Before leaving class today you must show me at least one reference source, two books from the main library collection and three academic journal articles related to your topic'. ('Constructivist, Social, and Situational Theories,' 2008 n.p.)

As Diane VanderPol, Jeanne M. Brown and Patricia Iannuzzi assert, academic libraries function especially well as learning 'laboratories.' Indeed, these authors consider today's academic library a remarkable place, a central location where college undergraduates go *especially* when they want to actively pursue their own learning. In the words of

VanderPol et al., libraries are 'places where students, with assistance and guidance, engage in hands-on practice to develop the skills and abilities to explore and discover, analyze and reflect, interpret, evaluate, and make connections' (2008: 12). Like laboratories in the sciences, academic libraries inherently foster 'an active learning environment for students to engage in inquiry and discovery, in groups, but with guidance' (12). Today's academic libraries offer teaching faculty an unsurpassed educational setting where any number of active learning experiences might immerse new students in high-quality research and exploration. As a result, these students can further not only their own disciplinary knowledge, but enhance their information literacy competency as well. Teaching faculty who work closely with their academic librarians to plan information literacy sessions in the library ensure that new undergraduates benefit not only from their professor's disciplinary knowledge, but also from the expertise of the information professionals who are trained to help novice researchers learn to successfully navigate the academic literature of any field.

Before taking a group of new undergraduates on a trip to the library, however, there are a few important issues to consider. After years of experimenting with various instructional settings and pedagogical techniques, it is clear that first-year students need to receive library instruction when they reach a critical point of need. Kuhlthau calls these points of need 'zones of intervention' and defines them as the 'area in which an information user can do with advice and assistance what he or she cannot do alone or can do only with great difficulty' (2004: 128–31). Consequently, the timing of library sessions must be carefully considered. To be most effective, information literacy education must be integrated into courses at a time during which students will find learning library research proficiencies most valuable. As a general rule, I have found that this most effective timing does *not* occur at the very start of a course. Teaching faculty who wish to schedule their library sessions early in their courses often say things such as, 'I want my students to really hit the ground running' or 'I want them to get into the library and start doing research right away.' When the course is filled with first-year students who require advice and assistance along virtually the entire research process I humbly submit that overly optimistic expectations such as these are likely to be dashed. If novice researchers do not have some type of course-based assignment that will immediately reinforce their learning by requiring them to practice and apply specific information literacy competencies, then a library session is really not worth doing. Mandy Lupton further endorses the importance of such intentionality when she writes, 'information literacy should be investigated as a learning activity, situated within a topic, course and discipline' (2008: 400). If new undergraduates are not asked to immediately try, repetitively demonstrate and diligently reflect upon the new library research concepts to which they are introduced, they will neither retain them nor will they be likely to transfer them to future academic projects (Nerz and Weiner, 2001: para. 12).

Fortunately for teaching faculty today, a great deal of information concerning the design of effective library research assignments, as well as a number of valuable information literacy assessment tools, is widely available on the Internet. At the time of the writing of this book, a Google search for ('information literacy' AND assignment*) returned 3,400,000 results; a similar search for ('information literacy' AND assessment) returned 5,850,000 results. Consequently, first-year teaching faculty with an interest in further exploring the many innovative ways in which library research assignments and information literacy assessment might be more intentionally and seamlessly integrated into their courses need only spend some time examining the profusion of examples already generously posted online. Individual academic librarians regularly post guidelines for creating effective library research assignments within the pages of their institution's library website. For example, one particularly nice online handout from Utah State University's Merrill-Cazier Library can be found at *http://it.usu.edu/fact/files/uploads/CreatingLibraryResearch.pdf*. Many academic librarians are also already hard at work assessing information literacy competency across their undergraduate populations. If members of the teaching faculty have an interest in this type of work, they should get in touch with the academic librarians at their individual institutions. As an example, perhaps the most well-known and rigorously tested information literacy assessment tool in use today is called *Project SAILS*. More information about this widely-used evaluation can be found at *https://www.projectsails.org/*.

The print literature of LIS is rife with examples for faculty to use as well. One particularly well-researched set of effective library assignment design principles appears in Hardesty's edited work, *The Role of the Library in the First College Year* (2007). In his chapter on information literacy and assignment design, Hardesty warns that creating high-quality library-based research assignments is critically important and that it is 'as complex as designing assignments to develop any other sophisticated ability in our students' (111). While he goes on to admit that creating high-quality library-based assignments is neither an exact nor a simple process, Hardesty does observe that successful first-year research assignments often share the following characteristics:

1. They are clear.

2. They are relevant to course goals.

3. They specify the source materials to be used.

4. They are feasible, both in terms of the library's resources and the scope of the topic chosen.

5. They are designed with and/or previewed by librarians.

6. They have been tested by instructors before being given to students.

7. They have been broken down into a series of shorter, sequenced tasks or assignments.

8. The assignments are linked closely in time to instruction.

9. They are appropriately challenging. (Hardesty, 2007: 111–16)

Of these nine qualities, I suggest that numbers five and six are likely to save the most time for teaching faculty. The importance of testing an assignment in the campus library *before* distributing it to new undergraduates cannot be overstated (point number 6). For some teaching faculty, such advice may be so obvious that it seems patronizing. Yet, in my own experience hastily designed library research assignments that have not been vetted in this manner continue to appear with surprising frequency. Such assignments require new undergraduates to use resources the library no longer owns (or owns in a different format), or provide dated (and therefore useless) instructions about how to access/use certain library tools, or ignore our newest and/or most relevant research tools, or necessitate that students use outmoded (and therefore extremely frustrating) research processes. It is important to be cognizant of the fact that the amount of angst such untested library assignments create among novice researchers is *not* insignificant. Teaching faculty who frequently test their own library research assignments help new students avoid a host of potentially distressing library encounters and go miles toward ensuring that the research project itself effectively promotes meaningful student learning. On the other hand, if teaching faculty choose to ignore all but suggestion number five (ask an academic librarian to preview any library research assignment), professors essentially eliminate the need for overly concerning themselves with the remaining eight characteristics. Academic librarians are extremely adept at identifying research assignment problem areas. We are eager to help teaching faculty brainstorm, plan, rethink or improve upon any assignment that might require an undergraduate to use their academic library. Lest teaching faculty be concerned that we academic librarians are going to immediately suggest major revisions to any and all library assignments that come before us, these faculty should rest assured that in *most* cases any changes that need to be made are likely to be minor. While certainly there are situations in which a librarian might *gently* suggest reframing or doing a larger-than-expected overhaul on an assignment, in my own experience these instances have been rare. Running a library project past a librarian usually takes little time, may result in easily manageable suggestions for improvement, and often eliminates a great deal of anxiety, frustration and disappointment for new student researchers and their busy professors.

Moving beyond Hardesty's thoughts on effective library assignment design, Barbara Ferrer Kenney provides an interesting framework for those instructors who might consider offering novice researchers a problem-based library 'experience' focused on individual information literacy competencies. Kenney suggests organizing this particular PBL session around the answers to five key questions and goes on to provide examples of her own responses to each.

- *What do you want the students to be able to do?* (Outcomes)

  - Use the library website and resources to find information
  - Use specific criteria to evaluate the information found

- *What does the student need to know?* (Curriculum)

  - The library website, a government website, a general database and evaluation criteria

- *What is the learning activity?* (Pedagogy)

  - Short introduction to the resources
  - Completion of a worksheet
  - Students working in teams using predetermined resources
  - Teams preselected as being either in favor of or against (a relevant topic)
  - A debriefing to ascertain the teams' positions and what information sources they used to come to their decisions

- *How will the students demonstrate the learning?* (Assessment)

  - Through their presentation and the evaluation of resources
  - Completion of a worksheet that will be graded

- *How will I know the student has done this well?* (Criteria)

  - The students clearly articulate a viable answer to the problem with evidence from authoritative sources. (Kenney, 2008: 389, emphasis added)

Kenney, like Hardesty, notes that developing meaningful research work for students is a challenging task. Carrying off an active library learning opportunity such as Kenney's PBL example above may not be for everyone. Yet, she also notes that this particular version of the library session also provides an innovative structure for collaboration and a good 'opportunity for students and faculty to experience library instruction in a new and dynamic way' (Kenney, 2008: 391).

Hardesty and Kenny's observations about library assignment and class design represent two unique contributions put forward by academic librarians in an effort to support professors who plan to integrate information literacy competencies into their courses. While their remarks are aimed at teaching faculty who are in the early stages of planning for somewhat larger instructional opportunities (an entire research project or information literacy session), librarians are also practiced at suggesting techniques for taking on complicated information literacy concepts on a more targeted level. One particularly succinct idea faculty might consider as a way of approaching a conversation about information literacy with new students comes from Misangyi Watts, (see Table 3.1 below).

Misangyi Watts' heuristic cleverly demonstrates how issues of information literacy integrate 'neatly with the concept of scholarly narratives, the very foundation of higher education' (2005: 350). As a result, this model provides a straightforward

Table 3.1 Integration of information literacy and scholarly narrative concept

Information Literacy Way of Learning	Scholarly Narratives
When is information needed?	Hypothesis, research questions
How can one find the information?	Methodology
Where can one find the information?	Review of the literature
How does one evaluate the information?	Interpretation, significance
What does one think of what one found?	Conclusion

Source: Misangyi Watts, 2005: 350.

way to begin conceptualizing a number of information literacy competencies for novice researchers. Additionally, directly tying information literacy to the scholarly work that is actively practiced by their own professors is a neat approach to reinforcing information literacy's importance to new undergraduates. Finally, once novice researchers see and understand the general correlations identified in Misangyi Watts' model, these students should have a reasonably good foundation that teaching faculty and academic librarians can continue to build upon as these students advance into more challenging discipline-specific research processes.

Valentine and Bernhisel (2008) offer yet another list of reminders for teaching faculty to reflect upon while creating research assignments for their new undergraduates. Here the focus shifts from distinguishing those information literacy competencies that first-year students need to develop further, to restating a number of the technological proficiencies Millennial high-school students often bring with them to college.

- Communication among and with students is easy.
- Digital access is no longer an issue.
- Plagiarism is easier to do.
- Use [students'] love of play [with technology] to turn distractions into assignments.
- Familiarity with a variety of easy to use tools means students can shift from being consumers of content to being creators.
- Students are not technologically savvy across all tools, only the ones they use. (Valentine and Bernhisel, 2008: 511)

It may seem somewhat surprising that today many librarians contribute to the academic literature on topics related to student technology use. Yet, if there is one place on campus where undergraduates regularly demonstrate the range of their technology skills, it is in their academic libraries. Though many of us did not go into librarianship with the dream of becoming avid technology connoisseurs, with rare exception, academic librarians today usually know at least something about the technologies students do and do not use to complete the research assignments given to them by their professors. Teaching faculty can benefit from this awareness in many ways. Talking with an academic librarian about matters such as electronic reserve, student plagiarism, Web 2.0 tools, online library tutorials, and the ever-changing array of electronic research sources available through the library is a great way to keep library research assignments current, relevant and appealing.

While Valentine and Bernhisel's findings reflect the influence technology has had on today's Millennials, Gilman (2009) is careful to reiterate the distinction between these students' purely technological prowess and their library savvy. Just as Valentine and Bernhisel maintain that 'students are not technologically savvy across all tools,' Gilman reminds teaching faculty not to 'assume that their students find themselves as much at home in the complex and daunting world of information as when they upload 25 photos from their iPhone to Facebook and text their friends' (2009: para. 5). Gilman is yet another academic librarian who understands that while many undergraduates may appear to be extremely 'computer-literate,' they are undeniably far from being 'research literate' (para. 4). It is with this important distinction in mind that he advocates for the following brief but pragmatic list of library-based actions:

- Spend a class period on search strategies.
- Take a tour.

- Reinforce the lesson with an assignment.
- Take it a step further ... do more than require a single [research-based] assignment. (Gilman, 2009: para. 11–14)

Gilman goes on to suggest that in an ideal world students would 'have multiple encounters with librarians' as a way of repositioning them to 'value the craft of research' (para. 15–16). Though his list is certainly less formal in tone than some of the others I have included in this book, its underlying message is analogous. Ultimately, Gilman is asking teaching faculty to consider the ways in which they might more actively involve the academic library in their teaching and in their students' learning.

If today's Millennial undergraduates are ever going to think of their work in the library as a 'craft,' then they must first be taught to think of it as anything but the tedious, time-consuming, unpleasant, old-fashioned requirement they seem to believe it is when they first arrive. By encouraging teaching faculty to remain flexible and to consider the variety of innovative formats student research projects might take, Rockman offers a few final suggestions for how faculty might further motivate their first-year students to see the value of being information literate.

> Assignments that are imaginative and focused on identifying, locating, accessing, evaluating, and integrating information into course content can lead to enhanced student learning by challenging students to think critically while engaging them in their own learning. These assignments can result in traditional written reports or less common creative expressions such as poster sessions, PowerPoint presentations, and Web pages, all of which can demonstrate students' mastery of information literacy principles through the

application of knowledge to a new setting. (Rockman, 2004a: 241)

Rockman's ideas above, as well as those that have been presented throughout this section, represent only a tiny fraction of the available advice provided by academic librarians about the development of effective library research experiences for first-year students. Even so, unless teaching faculty work closely with the academic librarians at their own institutions, it is highly unlikely (though understandable) that most faculty members have ever benefited from such guidance. As Hardesty reports, 'In graduate school, [doctoral students] learn the content of the discipline, develop an expertise in specialization and learn how to conduct research as presented in their dissertation' (2007: 110). Most graduate students do not learn how to teach undergraduates, especially the newest variety. As time goes by and these new faculty members do gain teaching experience, they also gain correspondingly increased institutional responsibilities. As a result, most members of today's teaching faculty have no background with, nor any extra time to read (much less think deeply about) the literature of disciplines much beyond their own. In fact, over the years many of my own friends and colleagues have shared the unfortunate truth with me that they never even realized librarians *had* a body of research-based disciplinary literature.

The lack of cross-disciplinary publishing has long been a communications problem for those of us who work in academic libraries. While some progress has been made in more recent years, the vast majority of research on issues related to information literacy, student learning and effective assignment design continues to appear within the literature of libraries. Because this work is so rarely read by our teaching faculty colleagues, I have included an appendix to this book. The appendix contains a bibliography purposely intended for non-librarian teaching faculty. This bibliography highlights research exclusively related to first-year student library researchers, successful information literacy pedagogical strategies and effective library assignment design. Information about these topics is, as I have already mentioned, prolifically available via the Internet and individual library websites (Hardesty, 2007: 118–19). Therefore, the citations included in this bibliography represent work that appears mainly in library-related publications (print or electronic). While it is not intended to be comprehensive in scope, this bibliography is meant to draw attention to at least a portion of the important information literacy work being done in the LIS field on course and program development, assignment design and student learning assessment. These are the kind of practical sources that teaching faculty might consider as a way to gather specific, strategic ideas for incorporating information literacy outcomes into their first-year courses.

The next step: advancing information literacy beyond the first year

ACRL's *Standards* document states that students 'need to have repeated opportunities for seeking, evaluating, and managing information gathered from multiple sources and discipline-specific research methods' throughout not only their undergraduate, but also their graduate school educations (ACRL, 2000: 5). While this book has primarily focused on those students who are newest to the academy, it is important not to underestimate the need for today's students to continually build and hone their information literacy competencies throughout their academic careers and beyond.

Long after completing their final academic course, today's students will be required to work and live in an increasingly complicated information landscape that will look entirely different than the one with which they are currently familiar. Brasley (2008) anticipates the complexity of this future landscape when she shares the following excerpt taken from a 2007 New Media Consortium and EDUCAUSE collaborative work titled the *Horizon Report* (*www.nmc. org/pdf/2007_Horizon_Report.pdf*): 'in a sea of user-created content, collaborative work, and instant access to information of varying quality, the skills of critical thinking, research, and evaluation are increasingly required to make sense of the world' (qtd. in Brasley, 2008: 86). In addition to the progressively changeable nature of information technologies, according to the *Standards*, 'the uncertain quality and expanding quantity of information pose large challenges for society' (ACRL, 2000: 2). As long as information technology continues to transform itself, maintaining information literacy competency will remain an ongoing challenge facing everyone. It should therefore be approached not as a skill to be mastered and never considered again (similar to riding a bike), but rather as an important, ongoing intellectual process that needs to be consistently exercised and developed (more like the work we must do to develop the muscles we use to ride that bike).

If today's institutions of higher education continue to see their central mission as preparing students to be lifelong learners, then their students will need consistent training about, regular practice with and a range of options for demonstrating their mastery of various information literacy competencies. ACRL's *Standards* maintain that 'Information literacy is a key component of, and contributor to, lifelong learning' (ACRL, 2000: 4). Those educational institutions that aspire to give Millennial students a 'foundation for continued growth throughout their careers, as well as in their roles as informed citizens and members of communities,' need to be more intentional about spreading meaningful opportunities for learning about and practicing information literacy competencies throughout their students' entire academic career (ACRL, 2000: 4). There are those who suggest that the onus for undertaking this task rests primarily on academic librarians.

> The need is for academic libraries to come to some consensus on the desired structure and content of a program that is comprehensive enough to ensure the information literacy training of every college and university student, and to convince the entire college/university community of the viability and effectiveness of that program. (Owusu-Ansah, 2003: 219)

While I understand the need for academic librarians to be active participants in and even ardent advocates for the creation of information literacy agendas at their institutions, I remain unconvinced that Owusu-Ansah's plan is an entirely realistic one. Without input from teaching faculty at *every* stage of the information literacy endeavor, academic librarians alone are unlikely to effect the kind of curricular change necessary to provide a consistent array of ongoing information literacy experiences from which students would benefit most. Unarguably, it is the members of the teaching faculty who make up the 'only group powerful enough on campus to make [information literacy] part of the curricular core' (Jenkins, 2005: 68). As this book has already noted, teaching faculty have an essential role to play when it comes to developing the information literacy skills of their students, if for no other reason than that 'no other group has a greater influence over the student body and its use of the library'

(Jenkins, 2005: 35). Breivik agrees, cautioning that 'when it comes to helping students master information literacy skills, the work has to center in the classroom' (2005: 26). Yet, if modern-day students are to wholly engage with the 'full range of information literacy skills,' then their instruction is going to require much 'more than a commitment from librarians and makeshift collaborations among well-meaning friends' (Fister, 2009: para. 6). Fister's statement implies that academic librarians and teaching faculty may still have quite a lot of work to do if we want to strengthen and extend our collaborative work. For while the information literacy movement has made progress, the establishment of many information literacy programs 'has been largely a process of experimentation and discovery,' which has only haphazardly made the most of atypical 'opportunities in an often indifferent or hostile environment with improvisation and make do' (Kohl, 1995: para. 3). If this is indeed the case, then without the commitment of teaching faculty from across our campuses, the likelihood of creating and sustaining strong information literacy programs is doubtful.

My own institution's information literacy approach serves as a good example of how long the process of developing a comprehensive, cohesive information literacy program can take. Twenty years ago my original library position was the first at this institution to include what was then called 'bibliographic instruction' as a formal job responsibility. While prior to my arrival there had been a number of ad hoc efforts to work with teaching faculty both in and out of their classrooms, teaching had never been considered any librarian's official responsibility. In 1991 40 percent of my position was committed to library instruction. Today, I cannot imagine this institution hiring *any* academic librarian who was not interested in devoting at least some significant portion of their position to information literacy education.

All of the librarians here currently teach and the majority teach quite a lot.

The most recent version of our first-year information literacy program has now been in place for five years. It is well organized and reasonably effectively assessed. While we could continue to improve further upon our assessment strategies, we do have solid participation statistics as well as good pre- and post-test learning data. Even these two smaller assessment pieces have helped us make adjustments to the program and to essentially monitor how things have been going. Of course there were *many* earlier iterations of the current program, each demonstrating varying levels of success. But today's student-centered, active-learning focus is so unlike the overwhelming 'here's how to do it' lectures that I frequently had to frantically rush through in the past that the program has truly been transformed. We believe that an increasing reliance on the constructivist learning model has served to not only improve student learning, but also to invigorate our teaching. For example, though I do still manage to occasionally lose a few first-year students, these less-than-motivated novice researchers are no longer able to *comfortably* fall asleep in my sessions. Today's novice researchers must move throughout the library building and engage with a variety of information resources in order to solve problems and present their findings. For the most part, those faculty who teach the college's first-year inquiry seminar have been supportive of the librarians' information literacy efforts on behalf of their newest students. After five years, we are pleased to report that we have 100 percent participation in the major component of our first-year student library program and many of our faculty members independently chose to have their classes go well beyond their initial library experiences. Regrettably, there are still a few faculty hold-outs who do not participate in the program as enthusiastically as we librarians wish they might. Nevertheless, our academic librarians and professors have engaged in a good deal of effective collaborative work, which has ensured that the process of developing this program over time has been a fundamentally rewarding one.

As with so many other information literacy programs, the remaining challenge at this institution is making the jump from being a program that mainly focuses on first-year undergraduates to one that consistently reaches students throughout their time here. Librarians are working toward this goal by intentionally connecting with individual academic department members through our librarian liaison program (each academic division has been assigned their own librarian). We also try to actively build upon the relationships that have developed with those teaching faculty who come to understand the importance of information literacy after teaching a first-year seminar. Currently there are departments on campus that have made good progress toward and, in some cases, have already instituted information literacy outcomes across their academic major. Though this group is small in number, word of their accomplishments has spread and the response to their plans has been positive. In addition to these department-level efforts, librarians hope to secure a formal place (similar to the one we have within the first-year seminar program) within the college's evolving capstone course program. Though the capstone courses are still being developed, librarians are optimistic about collaborating with the teaching faculty so that our senior students might have yet another formal opportunity to further advance their information literacy competencies before graduating. Without a doubt, this is an information literacy program that continues to be a work in progress. Perhaps it always will be.

According to Breivik, one of the main reasons some information literacy initiatives struggle to get up and running is likely due to the need for such far-reaching campus support. She explains further, writing that 'efforts to develop students' information literacy skills need to take place at the institutional, program, and classroom levels' (2005: 26). Because support must be garnered from within so many segments of an institution, the challenges to creating comprehensive, cohesive information literacy programming are many. Indeed, as academic librarians at the University at Albany quickly learned, such impediments are not insignificant.

> There are issues of buy-in by key players (faculty members, administrators, library administrators, and librarians), situating the program so that it is visible and effective, integrating information literacy with the general education program, and a host of other challenges that may be unique to a particular institution. [Challenges also exist based on] . . . the scalability of programs; professors and teaching assistants who are unaware of the benefits of information literacy; [and] the status of librarians. (Jacobson, 2004: 133–4)

No matter what size an institution is, hindrances such as these are serious and need to be carefully considered before support for a comprehensive information literacy curriculum is likely to gain traction. While academic librarians may be tempted to take over the entire planning process in order to avoid certain sticky concerns, this is a bad idea. As Hardesty cautions, just as 'the efforts [to create successful information literacy programs] will not succeed without librarians, the efforts cannot succeed if *only* librarians are involved' (2007: 173, emphasis added). Ultimately, there is no getting around the fact that there has to be good communication between and strong collaboration with teaching faculty if academic librarians want information literacy programming to really work for students.

Fortunately, there are a number of ways in which the call for a coherent information literacy agenda is increasing. For example, today several higher education accreditation agencies include specific language in their standards documents which reinforces the need for colleges and universities to include information literacy competencies in their curricula (ACRL, 2010a). Within the field of LIS itself, a recent report titled *The Value of Academic Libraries* goes to great lengths to encourage members of the profession to systematically focus on student learning. According to this document, in order 'to be successful contributors to their overarching institutions, academic libraries must maximize their contributions to student learning' (ACRL, 2010b: 37). While I've already noted that academic librarians cannot create thriving information literacy programs in isolation, this report further advances the notion that librarians must document the learning that happens in libraries. Whether students are taught information literacy proficiencies in a classroom, online, at the reference desk, or among the library stacks, academic librarians need to be more intentional about our assessment and reportage of this learning. We need to be well prepared with this data when support for the value of information literacy initiatives is questioned. Additionally, there are institutions where information literacy programming has been quite successful. At the University at Albany for example, Jacobson reports that while 'there have been some growing pains,' by and large their 'information literacy general education requirement is now a fact of life on campus' (2004: 136). In a chapter that describes the lengthy and often arduous route members of this university traveled in order to institute their across-the-board information literacy curriculum, Jacobson notes a number of the important lessons they learned during the process. Her tips are shared here in the hope that they might prove useful to members of institutions where curricular-level planning for information literacy may not be as far along.

- Make information literacy a campus concern.
- Involve all constituencies during implementation of the program.
- Have a small committee provide oversight.
- Do not leave out the librarians.
- Support instructors who are teaching information literacy.
- Support librarians who are supporting other faculty members.
- Evaluate information literacy courses and instruction and assess student learning. (Jacobson, 2004: 161–3)

Besides the University at Albany, today there exist a number of successful information literacy programs (Brasley, 2008; Hardesty, 2007: 177–262). Obviously, not all of these programmatic collaborations have the same broad curricular scope as Albany. Yet, these ventures continue to thrive, based on strong partnerships that have been built over time between 'library personnel and faculty, technologists, administrators and other higher education professionals' (Rockman, 2004b: 22). While it may take time and some effort, information literacy programming can and must work. As Brasley observes,

> rapid technological advances, changes in the academic library model, acceleration in teaching roles for

academic librarians, heightened awareness of information literacy by accrediting agencies, and pressure from the business community for sophisticated knowledge workers have all resulted in the value of information literacy being axiomatic to higher education. (Brasley, 2008: 73)

Developing an effective information literacy curriculum which consistently reaches every student and moves them through the research process at a pace appropriate to their learning style, cognition level, and disciplinary goals seems like an impossibly difficult proposal. Yet, it is important to remember that this work already happens, albeit in a less coordinated way, in classrooms and academic libraries everywhere. Because information technology is so pervasive and changeable, Millennial students face constant challenges to their information literacy competency simply by living their academic, work and daily lives. We, as academic librarians and teaching faculty, already do our best to help these students learn to research and think critically about their answers to questions whenever we can. However, now we must take a more focused educational approach. Educators need to be more intentional about articulating information literacy outcomes, teaching novice researchers this invaluable group of proficiencies and then requiring students to demonstrate mastery of these skills. To create successful information literacy programs at institutions large and small, we need to capitalize on the combined expertise of academic librarians and teaching faculty. If these partnerships are open, creative and thoughtful there is no reason to think they cannot result in a cohesive information literacy education plan that is innovative, clear and comprehensive.

Curzon writes that when 'students have mastery over information literacy, librarians and faculty have done their job as educators' (2004: 22). Certainly, there is no one-size-fits-all solution to the many challenges today's rapidly changing information technology landscape will create for the Millennials once they leave their institutions of higher education. But, while these students are on our campuses, academic librarians and teaching faculty need to make it possible for them 'to succeed in their education, to have a core skill that will give them a strategic advantage, and to build a lifelong skill that will make their lives richer' (Curzon, 2004: 44). This work will not be easy. Librarians and faculty members will need to be resourceful and persistent if we want to create the kind of valuable information literacy programs that will continue to do well over time at our individual institutions. However, once this work is under way and information literacy competency becomes part of the central educational mission of our institutions, we should be able to rest a little easier, knowing that we have equipped our students as best we can for their future information-rich lives.

One final note

As in most academic disciplines, the field of LIS has had its share of internal disagreements. One of the more notable discussions originally began due to 'controversies and uncertainties surrounding the conceptual delineation of information literacy' (Owusu-Ansah, 2003: 226; Snavely and Cooper, 1997). According to Owusu-Ansah, a number of disputes arose as a result of the external pressure being placed on academia to address information literacy 'even as controversies surrounding the exact meaning and implications of the concept' continued (2003: 219). Not only did librarians disagree about how to define the phrase, but once there seemed to be some general consensus about the definition, quarrels began about what to call this 'intellectual framework for understanding, finding, evaluating and using information ... through critical discernment and reasoning' (ACRL, 2000: 3). (Clearly *this* convoluted description was not likely to spawn an especially catchy moniker.) While most academic librarians today appear to be happy to leave the definition debate behind, some disagreement remains about what to actually name the concept of 'information literacy.' For example, alternative expressions such as 'information fluency,' 'infoliteracy' and 'information mediacy,' etc., can all be found within the LIS literature.

In writing this book, I chose to stick with the phrase 'information literacy' for two main reasons. First, and most importantly, this phrase remains the most widely used by practicing academic librarians today. Second, no matter how it is semantically parsed, as a concept, information literacy remains an exceedingly complex idea, one that simply cannot be entirely described by a single word or two.

> Information literacy education ventures into conceptual issues related to the very generation of information, the dynamics of its organization and processing and the implications of those processes for access, retrieval and use. It aims at delving into issues of copyright, intellectual property, and plagiarism. While bibliographic instruction provided a limited experience with the information universe, information literacy seeks to traverse the full length and breadth of that universe as it relates to the process of acquiring and using its products for learning and research. (Owusu-Ansah, 2003: 5)

Clearly, first-year students cannot become proficient in all things research-related overnight, no matter what academic librarians or teaching faculty might call that venerated status. As I have already noted, I believe developing information literacy competency takes place over time and on a lengthy continuum. Some students may advance more quickly, while others may need extra support and guidance as they build on whatever proficiencies they do have. Additionally, every new undergrad will eventually have unique research experiences as they gather, evaluate and use information from within their various academic disciplines. As a result of this inherent complexity, I see less value in arguing over what precise terminology should be used to describe so versatile a condition, than in ensuring today's college students are able to steadily progress toward it. I tend to side with Owusu-Ansah, who is unwilling to participate in 'a debate over definitions that often undermine[s] concentration on the development of concrete solutions aimed at achieving information literacy in higher education' (2003: 219). Yet, it is important to remember that academic librarians at individual institutions may justifiably hold differing views on this topic. The intent of my having introduced the subject here is basically to alert teaching faculty to the possibility that the academic librarians at their own institutions may use a different vocabulary to talk about their specific library instruction agendas. Having said that, it is important to reiterate that while academic librarians may not use the same terminology to talk about issues of information literacy, most are genuinely eager to help their teaching faculty 'create student-centered learning environments where inquiry is the norm, problem solving becomes the focus, and thinking critically is part of the process' (ACRL, 2000: 5). If librarians and teaching faculty agree that academic research experiences continue to have an important, meaningful effect on our first-year students and their ability to succeed, not only in college but beyond, then it really does not matter what we call information literacy or how we proceed, as long as we proceed together.

Conclusion

The importance of close collaboration between teaching faculty and academic librarians has been a key theme throughout this book. I do not recommend this working arrangement without due consideration. Collaborating with teaching faculty who are highly educated, accustomed to classroom autonomy and overwhelmingly busy, is by no means a simple assignment. Not to be outdone, we librarians have our own set of daunting work-related characteristics. Even the act of carving out a feasible meeting time to discuss information literacy can be a Herculean task. Nevertheless, as challenging as this work may be, my own experience has taught me that it can be exceedingly rewarding as well. Unsurprisingly, not every member of my own teaching faculty has embraced my collaborative overtures over the years. Yet, those with whom I have been able to connect continue to challenge my pedagogical expertise, work hard to create interesting courses and meaningful library assignments, and, best of all, these professors actively support their first-year students' research efforts in ways that are effective, creative and, dare I say it, exciting.

The new information literacy model represents a more sophisticated conceptualization of the librarian's role and relationship to the client, as well as to that of content design and delivery. With exposure to

> information literacy throughout the academic cycle
> as central to the development of lifelong learners,
> librarians now seek to foster and strengthen educational
> partnerships with academics. (Peacock, 2001: para 6)

Sustaining effective collaborative working relationships can take time and effort. Yet, in my own experience, collaborative work can take a variety of forms – some more involved than others. There are certain faculty members with whom I work so frequently that their students come to see me as an integral part of a course. In these instances, I often present multiple active-learning information literacy sessions throughout the course. I also conduct office visits with students in certain courses or, in some cases, I respond to and even grade portions of student research projects. I also collaborate with faculty in less involved ways. Quite a number of professors ask me to preview or provide research handouts, or to critique library assignments. Other faculty members ask me to create and present online library course web pages. Some faculty simply stop by my office to visit about their frustrations with or excitement over library assignments that either worked poorly or especially well with students. I work hard to keep my door open for such conversations and as a result have found that no matter how involved a collaboration gets, communicating and working with teaching faculty is absolutely the most professionally rewarding responsibility I perform as an academic librarian. This is *not* an unusual perspective to have among those of us in the profession. I share it here, because if this book achieves no other objective than to assure teaching faculty that academic librarians are *eager and willing* to be active partners in the educational missions of our institutions, then it will have been a great success. Stop by and talk with an academic librarian soon. Together we can help our newest Millennial students begin to build the 'intellectual framework for understanding, finding, evaluating, and using information,' that will sustain them far beyond their first college year (ACRL, 2000: 3).

Appendix: resources about integrating information literacy in the undergraduate classroom

Alfino, Mark, Michele Pajer, Linda Pierce, and Kelly O'Brien Jenks (2008) 'Advancing Critical Thinking and Information Literacy Skills in First Year College Students.' *College & Undergraduate Libraries* 15.1–2: 81–98. Print.

Armstrong, Jeanne (2010) 'Designing a Writing Intensive Course with Information Literacy and Critical Thinking Outcomes.' *Reference Services Review* 38.3: 445–57. Print.

Avery, Elizabeth Fuseler (ed.) (2003) *Assessing Student Learning Outcomes for Information Literacy Instruction in Academic Institutions.* Chicago, IL: ACRL. Print.

Bankert, Dabney A. and Melissa S. Van Vuuren (2008) 'Stranger in a Strange Land: The Undergraduate in the Academic Library, a Collaborative Pedagogy for Undergraduate Research.' *The CEA Forum* 37.1: n. pag. Web. 06 June 2010.

Bowles-Terry, Melissa, Erin Davis, and Wendy Holliday (2010) ' "Writing Information Literacy" Revisited: Application of Theory to Practice in the Classroom.' *Reference & User Services Quarterly* 49.3: 225–30. Print.

Brendle-Moczuk, Daniel (2006) 'Encouraging Students' Lifelong Learning through Graded Information Literacy Assignments.' *Reference Services Review* 34.4: 498–508. Print.

Burkhardt, Joanna M., Mary C. MacDonald, and Andrée J. Rathemacher (2003) *Teaching Information Literacy: 35 Practical Standards-based Exercises for College Students.* Chicago: ALA. Print.

Carder, Linda, Patricia Willingham, and David Bibb (2001) 'Case-based, Problem-based Learning Information Literacy for the Real World.' *Research Strategies* 18: 181–90. Print.

Caspers, Jean, and Steven Mark Bernhisel (2007) 'What Do Freshmen Really Know about Research? Assess before You Teach.' *Research Strategies* 20: 458–68. Print.

Daugherty, Alice L., and Michael F. Russo (2010) 'Reinforcing Critical Thinking and Information Literacy Skills through Assignment Design.' *Louisiana Libraries* 72.3: 26–9. Print.

Deitering, Anne-Marie, and Sara Jameson (2008) 'Step by Step through the Scholarly Conversation: A Collaborative Library/Writing Faculty Project to Embed Information Literacy and Promote Critical Thinking in First Year Composition at Oregon State University.' *College & Undergraduate Libraries* 15.1–2: 57–79. Print.

Dinkelman, Andrea L. (2010) 'Using Course Syllabi to Assess Research Expectations of Biology Majors: Implications for Further Development of Information Literacy Skills in the Curriculum.' *Issues in Science and Technology Librarianship* 60 (Winter 2010): n. pag. Web. *http://www. istl.org/10-winter/refereed3.html.*

Fink, Deborah (1986) 'What You Ask For is What You Get: Some Dos and Don'ts for Assigning Research Projects.' *Research Strategies* 4: 91–3. Print.

Gruber, Anne Marie, Mary Anne Knefel, and Paul Waelchli (2008) 'Modeling Scholarly Inquiry: One Article at a Time.' *College & Undergraduate Libraries* 15.1–2: 99–125. Print.

Harley, Bruce (2001) 'Freshmen, Information Literacy, Critical Thinking and Values.' *Reference Services Review* 29.4: 301–5. Print.

Hunt, Fiona, and Jane Birks (2004) 'Best Practices in Information Literacy.' *portal: Libraries and the Academy* 4.1: 27–39. Print.

Kenney, Barbara Ferrer (2008) 'Revitalizing the One-Shot Instruction Session Using Problem-Based Learning.' *Reference & User Services Quarterly* 47.4: 386–91. Print.

Keyser, Marcia W. (2000) 'Active Learning and Cooperative Learning: Understanding the Difference and Using Both Styles Effectively.' *Research Strategies* 17: 35–44. Print.

Keyser, Marcia W., and Laura R. Lucio (1999) 'Adding a Library Instruction Unit to an Established Course.' *Research Strategies* 16.3: 221–9. Print.

Lupton, Mandy (2008) 'Evidence, Argument and Social Responsibility: First-year Students' Experiences of Information Literacy when Researching an Essay.' *Higher Education Research & Development* 27.4: 399–414. Print.

Mackey, Thomas P., and Trudi Jacobson (2004) 'Integrating Information Literacy in Lower- and Upper-level Courses: Developing Scalable Models for Higher Education.' *JGE: The Journal of General Education.* 53.3–4: 201–24. Print.

Misangyi Watts, Margit (ed.) (2008) *Information Literacy: One Key to Education.* San Francisco: Jossey-Bass. Print. New Dir. for Teach. and Learn.

Nims, Julia K., Randal Baier, and Eric Bullard (eds.) (2003) *Integrating Information Literacy into the College Experience: Papers Presented at the Thirtieth National LOEX Library Instruction Conference.* 10–11 May 2002, Ypsilanti, MI: Pierian Press. Web. 10 Jan. 2011.

Nugent, Chris, and Roger Myers (2000) 'Learning by Doing: The Freshman-year Curriculum and Library Instruction.' *Research Strategies* 17: 147–55. Print.

Poyner, Ann (2005) *Enabling End-Users: Information Skills Training*. Stanton Harcourt, Oxford: Chandos Publishing Limited. Print.

Rockman, Ilene F. (ed.) (2004) *Integrating Information Literacy into the Higher Education Curriculum: Practical Models for Transformation*. San Francisco: John Wiley & Sons. Print.

Schuetz, Carol (2009) 'Not Your Parents' Chemistry Class: Integrating Library Skills into the Organic Chemistry Lab.' *College & Research Libraries News* 70.9: 522–5. Print.

Smith, Erin T., and Dorita F. Bolger (2010) 'Taking it Personally: Using Biography to Create a Common FYE Information Literacy Assignment.' *College & Research Libraries News* 71.5: 244–7. Print.

Spackman, Andy, and Leticia Camacho (2009) 'Rendering Information Literacy Relevant: A Case-based Pedagogy.' *The Journal of Academic Librarianship* 35.6: 548–54. Print.

References

Allen, Maryellen (2008) 'Promoting Critical Thinking Skills in Online Information Literacy Instruction Using a Constructivist Approach.' *College & Undergraduate Libraries* 15.1–2: 21–38. Print.

Alsop, Ron (2008) *The Trophy Kids Grow Up*. San Francisco: Jossey-Bass. Print.

American College Testing Program (ACT) (2009) *ACT National Curriculum Survey 2009*. Iowa City: ATC Inc. Web. 15 June 2010.

American Library Association (ALA) (1989) *Presidential Committee on Information Literacy. Final Report*. Chicago: ALA. Web. 05 May 2009. *http://www.ala.org/ala/mgrps/divs/acrl/publications/whitepapers/presidential.cfm*.

Anderson, Lorin, and David R. Krathwohl (eds.) (2001) *Taxonomy for Learning, Teaching, and Assessing: A Revision of Bloom's Taxonomy of Educational Objectives*. Abridged edn. New York: Longman. Print.

Association of American Colleges and Universities (AAC&U) (2002) *Greater Expectations: A New Vision for Learning as a Nation Goes to College*. National Panel Report. Washington, DC: AAC&U. 1–60. Print.

Association of College and Research Libraries (ACRL) (2000) *Information Literacy Competency Standards for Higher Education*. Chicago, IL: ALA, 2000. Web. 14 Apr. 2011. *http://www.ala.org/ala/mgrps/divs/acrl/standards/informationliteracycompetency.cfm*.

—— (2010a) *Accreditation*. Chicago, IL: ALA. Web. 30 Dec. 2010. *http://www.ala.org/ala/mgrps/divs/acrl/issues/ infolit/standards/accred/accreditation.cfm.*

—— (2010b) *Value of Academic Libraries: A Comprehensive Research Review and Report*. Res. by Megan Oakleaf. Chicago: ACRL. Web. 30 Dec. 2010. *http://www.acrl.ala .org/value.*

Badke, William B. (2005) 'Can't Get No Respect: Helping Faculty Understand the Educational Power of Information Literacy.' *Relationships between Teaching Faculty and Teaching Librarians* (ed.) Susan B. Kraat. Binghamton, NY: The Haworth Press. 63–80. Print.

Baker, Pam, and Renée R. Curry (2004) 'Integrating Information Competence into an Interdisciplinary Major.' *Integrating Information Literacy into the Higher Education Curriculum: Practical Models for Transformation*. Comp. Ilene F. Rockman and Assoc. San Francisco: Jossey-Bass. 93–132. Print.

Bankert, Dabney A., and Melissa S. Van Vuuren (2008) 'Stranger in a Strange Land: The Undergraduate in the Academic Library, a Collaborative Pedagogy for Undergraduate Research.' *The CEA Forum* 37.1: n. pag. Web. 06 June 2010.

Bauerlein, Mark (2009) *The Dumbest Generation: How the Digital Age Stupefies Young Americans and Jeopardizes Our Future*. New York: Jeremy P. Tarcher/Penguin. Print.

Bennett, Scott (2009) 'Libraries and Learning: A History of Paradigm Change.' *portal: Libraries and the Academy* 9.2: 181–97. Web. 25 Oct. 2010.

Beutter Manus, Sara J (2009) 'Librarian in the Classroom: An Embedded Approach to Music Information Literacy for First-Year Undergraduates.' *Notes* 66.2: 249–61. *Library Lit & Inf Full Text*. Web. 26 Oct. 2010.

Birmingham, Elizabeth, Luc Chinwongs, Molly Flaspohler, Carly Hearn, Danielle Kranvig and Ronda Portmann (2008) 'First-Year Writing Teachers, Perceptions of Students' Information Literacy Competencies, and a Call for a Collaborative Approach.' *Communications in Information Literacy* 2.1: 6–24. Web. 04 May 2010.

Bowles-Terry, Melissa, Erin Davis, and Wendy Holliday (2010) ' "Writing Information Literacy" Revisited: Application of Theory to Practice in the Classroom.' *Reference & User Services Quarterly* 49.3: 225–30. Print.

Brasley, Stephanie Sterling (2008) 'Effective Librarian and Discipline Faculty Collaboration Models for Integrating Information Literacy into the Fabric of an Academic Institution.' *Information Literacy: One Key to Education.* Ed. Margit Misangyi Watts. San Francisco: Jossey-Bass. 71–88. Print.

Breivik, Patricia Senn (2005) '21st Century Learning and Information Literacy.' *Change* 37.2: 20–7. Print.

Brown, Malcolm (2005) 'Learning Spaces.' *Educating the Net Generation.* Eds. Diana G. Oblinger and James L. Oblinger. Boulder, CO: EDUCAUSE. 12.1–12.22. Web. 25 May 2010. *http://www.educause.edu/ir/library/pdf/pub7101.pdf.*

Bruce, Christine Susan (2004) 'Information Literacy as a Catalyst for Educational Change: A Background Paper.' *Lifelong Learning: Whose Responsibility and What Is Your Contribution?* 3rd International Lifelong Learning Conference. Yeppoon, Central Queensland, Australia: Central Queensland University. 13–16 June. Web. 01 June 2010. *http://eprints.qut.edu.au/4977/1/4977_1.pdf.*

Buckingham, David (ed.) (2008) *Youth, Identity and Digital Media.* Cambridge, MA: The MIT Press. Web. 04 May 2010.

Bundy, Alan (2004) 'Beyond Information: The Academic Library as Educational Change Agent.' 7th International

Bielefeld Conference. Bielefeld University, Germany, 3 Feb. 2004. Web. 25 May 2010.

Burkhardt, Joanna M., Mary C. MacDonald, and Andrée J. Rathemacher (2003) *Teaching Information Literacy: 35 Practical Standards-based Exercises for College Students*. Chicago, IL: ALA. Print.

Burton, Vicki Tolar and Scott A. Chadwick (2000) 'Investigating the Practices of Student Researchers: Patterns of Use and Criteria for Use of Internet and Library Sources.' *Computers and Composition* 17: 309–28. Print.

Byerly, Gayla, Annie Downey, and Lilly Ramin (2006) 'Footholds and Foundations: Setting Freshmen on the Path to Lifelong Learning.' *Reference Services Review* 34.4: 589–98. Print.

Carder, Linda, Patricia Willingham, and David Bibb (2001) 'Case-based, Problem-based Learning: Information Literacy for the Real World.' *Research Strategies* 18: 181–90. Print.

Caspers, Jean and Steven Mark Bernhisel (2007) 'What Do Freshmen Really Know about Research? Assess before You Teach.' *Research Strategies* 20: 458–68. Print.

Connaway, Lynn Silipigni, Marie L. Radford, Timothy J. Dickey, Jocelyn De Angelis Williams, and Patrick Confer (2008) 'Sense-Making and Synchronicity: Information-Seeking Behaviors of Millennials and Baby Boomers.' *Libri* 58: 123–35. Print.

'Constructivist, Social, and Situational Theories' (2008) *Learning Theories Knowledgebase*. Learning-Theories.com. Web. 27 Dec. 2010. *http://www.learning-theories.com*.

CSU-SUNY-CUNY Joint Committee (1997) *The Academic Library in the Information Age: Changing Roles*. Seal Beach, CA: Consortium for Educational Technology for University Systems. Print. Discussion Ser.

Curzon, Susan Carol (2004) 'Developing Faculty-Librarian Partnerships in Information Literacy. Integrating Information Literacy into the Higher Education Curriculum: Practical Models for Transformation.' Comp. Ilene F. Rockman and Assoc. San Francisco: Jossey-Bass. 29–45. Print.

DaCosta, Jacqui Weetman (2010) 'Is There an Information Literacy Skills Gap to Be Bridged? An Examination of Faculty Perceptions and Activities Relating to Information Literacy in the United States and England.' *College & Research Libraries* 71.3: 203–22. Print.

Economist, The (2010) 'Data, Data Everywhere.' *The Economist* 394.8671: n. pag. *Academic Search Premier.* Web. 5 Jan. 2011.

Elmborg, James (2006) 'Critical Information Literacy: Implications for Instructional Practice.' The *Journal of Academic Librarianship* 32.2: 192–9. Print.

Fister, Barbara (1992) 'The Research Processes of Undergraduate Students.' *The Journal of Academic Librarianship*. 18.3: 163–9. Print.

—— (1995) 'Connected Communities: Encouraging Dialogue between Composition and Bibliographic Instruction.' *Writing-Across-the-Curriculum and the Academic Library.* Ed. Jean Sheridan. Westport, CT: Greenwood Press. 33–52. Print.

—— (2009) 'Fostering Information Literacy Through Faculty Development.' *Library Issues* 29.4: n. pag. Print.

Fitzgerald, Mary Ann (2004) 'Making the Leap from High School to College.' *Knowledge Quest* 32.4: 19–4. Print.

Foster, Andrea L. (2006) 'Students Fall Short on "Information Literacy" Education Testing Service's Study Finds.' *The Chronicle of Higher Education* 53.10: A36. *The Chronicle of Higher Education Online.* Web. 17 June 2010.

Foster, Nancy Fried, and Susan Gibbons (eds.) (2007) *Studying Students: The Undergraduate Research Project at the University of Rochester.* Chicago, IL: ACRL. Web. 16 Dec. 2010. *http://docushare.lib.rochester.edu/docushare/dsweb/View/Collection-4436.*

Geck, Caroline (2006) 'The Generation Z Connection: Teaching Information Literacy to the Newest Net Generation.' *Teacher Librarian* 33.3: 19–23. Print.

George, Mary W. (1988) 'What Do College Librarians Want Freshmen to Know? My Wish List.' *RS: Research Strategies* 6: 189. Print.

Gilman, Todd (2009) 'Not Enough Time in the Library.' *The Chronicle of Higher Education.* 14 May 2009. Web. 4 May 2010.

Given, Lisa M., and Heidi Julien (2005) 'Finding Common Ground: An Analysis of Librarians' Expressed Attitudes Towards Faculty.' *The Reference Librarian* 89/90: 25–38. Print.

Gross, Melissa and Don Latham (2009) 'Undergraduate Perceptions of Information Literacy: Defining, Attaining, and Self-Assessing Skills.' *College & Research Libraries* 70.4: 336–50. Print.

Hall, Russell A. (2008) 'The "Embedded" Librarian in a Freshman Speech Class.' *College & Research Library News* 69.1: 28–30. Print.

Hardesty, Larry (1995) 'Faculty Culture and Bibliographic Instruction: An Exploratory Analysis – The Library and Undergraduate Education.' *Library Trends* 44.2: n. pag. Web. 07 May 2010.

——, ed. (2007) *The Role of the Library in the First College Year.* Columbia, SC: University of South Carolina, National Resource Center for the First-Year Experience and Students in Transition. Print.

Harley, Bruce (2001) 'Freshmen, Information Literacy, Critical Thinking and Values.' *Reference Services Review* 29.4: 301–5. Print.

Head, Alison J. and Michael B. Eisenberg (2009) *Finding Context: What Today's College Students Say about Conducting Research in the Digital Age*. Project Information Literacy Progress Report. Seattle, WA: The Information School, University of Washington. 04 February 2009. 1–18. Web. 11 May 2010. *http://projectinfolit.org/pdfs/PIL_ProgressReport_2_2009.pdf*.

—— (2010) *Truth Be Told: How College Students Evaluate and Use Information in the Digital Age*. Project Information Literacy Progress Report. Seattle, WA: The Information School, University of Washington. 1 Nov. 2010. 1–71. Web. 14 Dec. 2010. *http://projectinfolit.org/pdfs/PIL_Fall2010_Survey_FullReport1.pdf*.

Herring, Susan C. (2008) 'Questioning the Generational Divide: Technological Exoticism and Adult Constructions of Online Youth Identity.' *Youth, Identity, and Digital Media*. Ed. David Buckingham. Cambridge, MA: The MIT Press. 71–92. Print.

Howe, Neil and William Strauss (2007) *Millennials Go to College*. 2nd ed. Great Falls, VA: LifeCourse Associates. Print.

Hunt, Fiona and Jane Birks (2004) 'Best Practices in Information Literacy.' *portal: Libraries and the Academy* 4.1: 27–39. Print.

Mizuko Ito, Sonja Baumer, Matteo Bittanti, Danah Boyd, Rachel Cody, Becky Herr-Stephenson, Heather A. Horst, Patricia G. Lange, Dilan Mahendran, Katynka Z. Martinez, C. J. Pascoe, Dan Perkel, Laura Robinson, Christo Sims and Lisa Tripp (2010) *Hanging Out, Messing Around, and Geeking Out: Kids Living and*

Learning with New Media. Cambridge, MA: The MIT Press. Print.

Jacobs, Heidi L. M. and Dale Jacobs (2009) 'Transforming the One-Shot Library Session into Pedagogical Collaboration: Information Literacy and the English Composition Class.' *Reference & User Services Quarterly* 49.1: 72–82. *Library Lit & Inf Full Text*. Web. 26 Oct. 2010.

Jacobson, Trudi E. (2004) 'Meeting Information Literacy Needs in a Research Setting.' *Integrating Information Literacy into the Higher Education Curriculum: Practical Models for Transformation*. Comp. Ilene F. Rockman and Assoc. San Francisco: Jossey-Bass. 133–64. Print.

Jenkins, Paul O. (2005) *Faculty-Librarian Relationships*. Oxford: Chandos Publishing. Print.

Kenedy, Robert, and Vivienne Monty (2008) 'Dynamic Purposeful Learning in Information Literacy.' *Information Literacy: One Key to Education* Ed. Margit Misangyi Watts. San Francisco: Jossey-Bass. 89–99. Print. New Dir. for Teach. and Learn.

Kenney, Barbara Ferrer (2008) 'Revitalizing the One-Shot Instruction Session Using Problem-Based Learning.' *Reference & User Services Quarterly* 47.4: 386–91. Print.

Keyser, Marcia W. (2000) 'Active Learning and Cooperative Learning: Understanding the Difference and Using Both Styles Effectively.' *Research Strategies* 17: 35–44. Print.

Knutson, Karla (2010) *Unit 2: What Do I Want to Know about the World? How Can Writing Help Me Explore the World? Paper 2: The Researched Essay*. Concordia College, Moorhead, MN. Print.

Kohl, David K. (1995) 'As Time Goes By . . .: Revisiting Fundamentals.' *Library Trends* 44.2: n. pag. Web. 26 May 2010.

Kuh, George D., Polly D. Boruff-Jones, and Amy E. Mark (2007) 'Engaging Students in the First College Year:

Why Academic Librarians Matter.' *The Role of the Library in the First College Year*. Ed. Larry Hardesty. Columbia, SC: University of South Carolina, National Resource Center for The First Year Experience and Students in Transition. 17–27. Print. First-Year Experience Mon. Ser.

Kuhlthau, Carol Collier (2004) *Seeking Meaning: A Process Approach to Library and Information Services*. 2nd ed. Westport, CT: Libraries Unlimited. Print.

Kuhlthau, Carol Collier, Jannica Heinström, and Ross J. Todd (2008) 'The "Information Search Process" Revisited: Is the Model Still Useful?' *Information Research* 13.4: n. pag. Web. 7 June 2010.

Kunkel, Lilith R., Susan M. Weaver, and Kim N. Cook (1996) 'What Do They Know?: An Assessment of Undergraduate Library Skills.' *The Journal of Academic Librarianship* 22.6: 430–4. Print.

Leamnson, Robert (2003) *Thinking about Teaching and Learning: Developing Habits of Learning with First Year College and University Students*. Sterling, VA: Stylus Publishing. Print.

Leckie, Gloria J. (1996) 'Desperately Seeking Citations: Uncovering Faculty Assumptions about the Undergraduate Research Process.' *The Journal of Academic Librarianship* 22.3: 201–8. Print.

Levitov, Deborah (2004) 'Defining Information Literacy.' *Nebraska Library Association Quarterly* 35. 4: 25–7. Print.

Lippincott, Joan K. (2005) 'Net Generation Students and Libraries.' *Educating the Net Generation*. Eds. Diana G. Oblinger and James L. Oblinger. Boulder, CO: EDUCAUSE. 13.1–13.15. Web. 25 May 2010. *http://www.educause.edu/ir/library/pdf/pub7101.pdf*.

Livingstone, Sonia (2008) 'Internet Literacy: Young People's Negotiation of New Online Opportunities.' *Digital Youth, Innovation, and the Unexpected*. Ed. Tara McPherson.

The John D. and Catherine T. MacArthur Foundation Series on Digital Media and Learning. Cambridge, MA: The MIT Press. 101–21. Print.

Lorenzen, Michael (2001) 'A Brief History of Library Information in the United States of America.' *Illinois Libraries* 83.2: 8–18. Print.

Lupton, Mandy (2008) 'Evidence, Argument and Social Responsibility: First-year Students' Experiences of Information Literacy When Researching an Essay.' *Higher Education Research & Development* 27.4: 399–414. Print.

Malone, Debbie and Carol Videon (2007) 'Models of Library Instruction for First-Year Students.' *The Role of the Library in the First College Year*. Ed. Larry Hardesty. Chicago: ALA; Columbia, SC: National Resource Center for The First-Year Experience and Students in Transition. 51–68. Print.

Malvasi, Martina, Catherine Rudowsky, and Jesus M. Valencia (2009) *Library Rx: Measuring and Treating Library Anxiety*. Chicago: ALA. Print.

McGuinness, Claire (2006) 'What Faculty Think – Exploring the Barriers to Information Literacy Development in Undergraduate Education.' *The Journal of Academic Librarianship* 32.6: 573–82. Print.

McInnis, Raymond G. (1978) *New Perspectives for Reference Service in Academic Libraries*. Westport, CT: Greenwood. Print.

McLoughlin, Catherine, and Mark J.W. Lee (2008) 'The Three Ps of Pedagogy for the Networked Society: Personalization, Participation, and Productivity.' *International Journal of Teaching and Learning in Higher Education* 20.1: 10–27. Web. 2 July 2010.

Meyers, Eric M., Karen E. Fisher, and Elizabeth Marcoux (2009) 'Making Sense of an Information World: The Everyday-life Information Behavior of Preteens.' *The Library Quarterly* 79.3: 301–14. Print.

Miller, William and Steven Bell (2005) 'A New Strategy for Enhancing Library Use: Faculty-Led Information Literacy Instruction.' *Library Issues* 25.5: n. pag. Web. 12 May 2010.

Misangyi Watts, Margit (2005) 'The Place of the Library versus the Library as Place.' *Challenging and Supporting the First-Year Student: A Handbook for Improving the First Year of College.* Eds. M. Lee Upcraft, John N. Gardner, and Betsy O. Barefoot. San Francisco: Jossey-Bass. 339–55. Print.

Montgomery, Kathryn C. (2007) *Generation Digital: Politics, Commerce, and Childhood in the Age of the Internet.* Cambridge, MA: The MIT Press. Print.

Nerz, Honora F., and Suzanne T. Weiner (2001) 'Information Competencies: A Strategic Approach.' *Proceedings of the 2001 American Society for Engineering Annual Conference and Exposition, June 24 – 27, 2001: Session 2241.* N. p.: American Society for Engineering Education. N. pag. Web.

Nugent, Chris and Roger Myers (2000) 'Learning By Doing: The Freshman-year Curriculum and Library Instruction.' *Research Strategies* 17: 147–55. Print.

Online Computer Library Center (OCLC) (2002) 'How Academic Librarians Can Influence Students' Web-Based Information Choices.' White Paper. Dublin, OH: OCLC Online Computer Library Center, Inc. Web. 25 Oct. 2010.

—— (2006) *College Students' Perceptions of Libraries and Information Resources.* Dublin, OH: OCLC Inc. Print.

Onwuegbuzie, Anthony J., Qun G. Jiao, and Sharon L. Bostic (2004) *Library Anxiety: Theory, Research, and Applications.* Ser. Eds. Ronald R. Powell and Lynn Westbrook. Lanham, MD: The Scarecrow Press. Print. Res. Meth. in Lib. and Info. Studies.

Orme, William A. (2008) 'Information Literacy and First-Year Students.' *Information Literacy: One Key to Education* Ed. Margit Misangyi Watts. San Francisco: Jossey-Bass. 63–70. Print. New Dir. for Teach. and Learn.

Oseguera, Leticia (2007) 'How First-Year College Students Use Their Time: Implications for Library and Information Literacy Instruction.' *The Role of the Library in the First College Year*. Ed. Larry Hardesty. Columbia, SC: University of South Carolina, National Resource Center for the First-Year Experience and Students in Transition. 29–47. Print.

Owusu-Ansah, Edward K. (2003) 'Information Literacy and the Academic Library: A Critical Look at a Concept and the Controversies Surrounding It.' *The Journal of Academic Librarianship* 29.4: 219–30. Print.

Palfrey, John and Urs Gasser (2008) *Born Digital: Understanding the First Generation of Digital Natives*. New York: Basic Books. Print.

Pattillo, Gary (2010) 'Fast Facts.' *College & Research Libraries News* 71.5: 276. Print.

Peacock, Judith (2001) 'Teaching Skills for Teaching Librarians: Postcards from the Edge of the Educational Paradigm.' *Australian Library and Information Association (AARL)* 32.1: n. pag. Web. 25 May 2010.

Pletka, Bob (2007) *Educating the Net Generation: How to Engage Students in the 21st Century*. Santa Monica, CA: Santa Monica Press. Print.

Pritchard, Peggy A. (2010) 'The Embedded Science Librarian: Partner in Curriculum Design and Delivery.' *Journal of Library Administration* 50.4: 373–96. *Library Lit & Inf Full Text*. Web. 26 Oct. 2010.

Rentfrow, Daphnée (2008) 'Groundskeepers, Gatekeepers, and Guides: How to Change Faculty Perceptions of Librarians and Ensure the Future of the Research Library.' *No Brief Candle: Reconceiving Research Libraries for the 21st Century*. CLIR Publication No. 142. Washington, DC: Council on Library and Information Resources. 58–65. Print.

Rockman, Ilene F. (2004a) 'Conclusion: Continuing the Dialogue.' *Integrating Information Literacy into the Higher Education Curriculum: Practical Models for Transformation.* Comp. Ilene F. Rockman and Assoc. San Francisco: Jossey-Bass. 237–50. Print.

——— (2004b) 'Introduction.' *Integrating Information Literacy into the Higher Education Curriculum: Practical Models for Transformation.* Comp. Ilene F. Rockman and Assoc. San Francisco: Jossey-Bass. 1–28. Print.

——— (2004c) 'Successful Strategies for Integrating Information Literacy into the Curriculum.' *Integrating Information Literacy into the Higher Education Curriculum: Practical Models for Transformation.* Comp. Ilene F. Rockman and Assoc. San Francisco: Jossey-Bass. 47–69. Print.

Sanger, Larry (2010) 'Individual Knowledge in the Internet Age.' *EDUCAUSE Review* 45.2 (March/April): n. pag. Web. 03 May 2010.

Snavely, Loanne (2008) 'Global Education Goals, Technology, and Information Literacy in Higher Education.' *Information Literacy: One Key to Education* Ed. Margit Misangyi Watts. San Francisco: Jossey-Bass. 35–46. Print. New Dir. for Teach. and Learn.

Snavely, Loanne and Natasha Cooper (1997) 'The Information Literacy Debate.' *The Journal of Academic Librarianship* 23.1: 9–14. Print.

Spackman, Andy and Leticia Camacho (2009) 'Rendering Information Literacy Relevant: A Case-Based Pedagogy. *The Journal of Academic Librarianship* 35.6: 548–54. Print.

Spence, Larry (2004) 'The Usual Doesn't Work: Why We Need Problem-Based Learning.' *portal: Libraries and the Academy* 4.4: 485–93. Print.

Swanson, Troy (2006) 'Information Literacy, Personal Epistemology, and Knowledge Construction: Potential and Possibilities.' *College & Undergraduate Libraries* 13.3: 93–112. Print.

Tapscott, Don (2009) *Grown Up Digital: How the Net Generation is Changing the World*. New York: McGraw-Hill. Print.

Twomey, Lisa (2010) Personal Interview. 19 Oct. 2010.

Upcraft, M. Lee, John N. Gardner, and Betsy O. Barefoot (2005). San Francisco, CA: Jossey-Bass. 339–55. Print.

Valentine, Barbara and Steven Bernhisel (2008) 'Teens and Their Technologies in High School and College: Implications for Teaching and Learning.' *The Journal of Academic Librarianship* 34.6: 502–12. Print.

VanderPol, Diane, Jeanne M. Brown, and Patricia Iannuzzi (2008) 'Reforming the Undergraduate Experience.' *Information Literacy: One Key to Education*. Ed. Margit Misangyi Watts. San Francisco: Jossey-Bass. 5–15. Print. New Dir. for Teach. and Learn.

Van Scoyoc, Anna M. (2003) 'Reducing Library Anxiety in First-year Students.' *Reference & User Services Quarterly* 42.4: 329–41. Print.

Weiler, Angela (2004) 'Information-Seeking Behavior in Generation Y Students: Motivation, Critical Thinking, and Learning Theory.' *The Journal of Academic Librarianship* 31.1: 46–53. Print.

Whitehurst, Angela P. (2010) 'Information Literacy and Global Readiness: Library Involvement Can Make a World of Difference.' *Behavioral & Social Sciences Librarian* 29.3: 207–32. *Library Lit & Inf Full Text*. Web. 26 Oct. 2010.

Wilson, Lizabeth A. (2004) 'What A Difference A Decade Makes: Transformation in Academic Library Instruction.' *Reference Source Review* 32.4: 338–46. Print.

Index